D0762233

THE HOPE OF A NEW WORLD

THE HOPE OF A NEW WORLD

BY

WILLIAM TEMPLE

Essay Index Reprint Series

 BOOKS FOR LIBRARIES PRESS
FREEPORT, NEW YORK

First Published 1940
Reprinted 1970

INTERNATIONAL STANDARD BOOK NUMBER:
0-8369-1778-2

LIBRARY OF CONGRESS CATALOG CARD NUMBER:
74-121507

PRINTED IN THE UNITED STATES OF AMERICA

CONTENTS

I

THE HOPE OF A NEW WORLD

I

What is wrong with the old world?

IF we are to hope and work for a new world with any confidence, we must have as clear a notion as possible about the faults of the old world. Of course it is quite clear that a great deal was wrong with it; otherwise it could not have plunged again into the catastrophe of general war. But it is not very useful to see or to say this, unless one sees where the wrong actually lay and still lies. About one part of the answer to this question, I have no doubts whatever; and about another part I have an equally strong personal assurance, though I find that some who agree with the first chapter of my jeremiad, disagree with me about the second.

The summary of the first chapter is this: we have neglected God and His laws. Historians of the future will admire very much about the nineteenth century and its products in the early decades of this century. But they will, I am sure, express a bewildered astonishment at the attitude to God and to faith in God, which increasingly prevailed in that period—I mean the attitude which regards God and faith in God as an optional extra, so to speak, to be added according to taste when the requirements of a decent human life have been met—the attitude often expressed in the astonishingly silly saying that a man's religion is a private affair between him and his Maker. The prevalence of this childishly superficial attitude has been possible only because we have inherited a civilization largely permeated by principles which derive all their validity from faith in God, and indeed in God as Christians have learnt to understand Him, yet have not troubled to know on what those principles rest. Those principles were so firmly rooted in the minds of our fathers and grand-fathers that they took them for granted, even when they ceased to attend to their source. It has needed the shock of this war, and the perception of what is at stake in it, to call the attention of multitudes once more to the real foundation of the way of life which we are fighting to preserve; and there are multitudes more for whom that has not yet happened even now.

The prevalent feeling of our countrymen, when they contemplate the Nazi tyranny, is a sense of outrage. It seems incredible that men should really believe what they have proclaimed as their convictions. It is not what they do that horrifies us so much as what they preach. People often say to a preacher: "Practise what you preach." That is a very wholesome prod for the preacher's conscience; but if the preacher in fact preaches nothing more than he can practise, he is preaching very badly. The trouble with the Nazis is not that they do not practise what they preach; it is that they do preach what they practise. Their standards are perverted; their right is our wrong.

Now that is horrifying. For a long time we could not believe it. They told us very plainly what they believed and what, accordingly, they meant to do. But we went on hoping that if only we gave them a little relief here, and a small concession there, they would turn out to be decent human beings after all. Of course we know now that when Hitler sent his troops into the Rhineland we ought to have driven them out again at once. I do not mean that we ought to have fought for every clause of the Treaty of Versailles; in fact, we ought to have modified parts of it a great deal earlier than that, and then perhaps Hitler would never have won his power at all. But though we are partly responsible for the opportunity which the evil genius of Germany has seized, we ought, as we see now, to have resisted that evil genius from the outset. Our failure to do this, and our failure to recognize the evil thing for what it was, had one chief cause. We had settled down into a comfortable enjoyment of a life which sprang from, and could only be safeguarded by, a living Christian faith. We thought what we had learnt to value must be prized by all sane men. When we find these things, which are so precious to us, despised by others, and look for the ground of our confidence in them, we can, in fact, find this nowhere except in God as Christ has made Him known.

So we come back to the paradox of modern English culture, which is largely Christian in quality, yet regards faith in God as a dispensable indulgence. This reaches its climax in our educational system. We have supposed that it is possible to provide education which is religiously neutral, to which religion can then be added in greater or less measure. But, in fact, an education which is not religious is atheistic; there is no middle way. If you give to children an account of the world from which God is left out, you are teaching them to understand the world without reference to God. If He is then introduced, He is an excrescence. He becomes an appendix to His own creation.

Now if God exists at all, it is obvious that He is the most important of all existing things; we can understand nothing properly until we see it in its relation to God and His purpose. If we are to save those precious things, which we are fighting to preserve from obliteration in the overflowing flood of Nazi barbarism, our first need is to return to God and see ourselves as

His creatures, dependent in all things upon Him.

It was natural that neglect of God should lead to violation of His law. I am not now thinking of the Ten Commandments but of that general law, or order of things, which is the framework of our lives and found particular expression, adapted to the circumstances of another age, in the economic legislation of the Old Testament. We need to appreciate again not only the profound wisdom of that legislation for its own time, but the abiding importance of its underlying principle. For that principle is precisely the allowing of free play to individual initiative in such a way that no man acquires the right to possess, to exploit or to hold down his neighbour.

In the next two talks of this series, I hope to say something more about the way in which we must correct our neglect of God; in the two which follow those, my subject will be the way of obedience in our public life. But now I go on with my account of what is wrong with the old world by pointing to some results of our neglect both of God and of His laws.

To a great many people the traditional language of Christians has become unmeaning.[1] It does not fit in with their way of looking at life. They scarcely know what we mean by the word sin, supposing sin to consist in consciously doing what is known or believed to be wrong. But this is only one part of the whole great fact of sin—the visible part, so to speak. It is the

[1] See below, " Evangelism in Our Time," pp. 105-118.

symptom, not the disease; the inflammation, not the poison. All is sin that falls short of God's will for it, and the essence of man's sin is his self-centredness. But this is forgotten, and because people have so scanty an understanding of sin they attach no meaning whatever to redemption. The result is that when we preach the Gospel, we are, so to speak, shooting over their heads; it makes no impact on them.

But there is something of which many people are acutely aware, and of which a great many more quite easily become aware; this is futility and that baffled irritation which we have learnt to call " frustration ". It became manifest in the last war, and is now manifest again, that what gives meaning and value to life is a cause to which life can be devoted. Life finds its value in a cause for which it is worth while to die. No man who is actually serving such a cause, however small his own contribution to it, ever feels frustrated. At present we have all found such a cause. It is worth while to die at the hands of the barbarous Nazi tyranny, if we may thus do something to secure justice and freedom for the generations to come.

It is a characteristic of war that it provides sharp alternatives; we may have to choose between loyalty with death on one side, and life with shame on the other. The right choice is glorious, and therefore comparatively easy. It is easier to die for a cause than to live for it; living for it means the setting aside of pleasure and self-interest in a host of little choices, where there is no glory, at least in men's eyes, on the one side, and no open shame on the other. Yet if life is to keep for us its dignity and value, we must find something to live and die for in peace as in war.

Some find this in the pursuit of knowledge or of beauty; but we cannot all be scientists or artists; and even for them, their chosen ideals never cover the whole of life. Nothing does that except the purpose of God. The one sovereign cure for a sense of futility and frustration is faith in God. If anyone's faith in God were complete, so that he trusted God with his whole being, that would give direction and meaning to every moment of his time and every jot of his activity; and a man has this sense of direction and meaning in life just so far as he really does believe and trust in God.

We had let that slip into the background. Is it not true that a great number of us had come to think of comfort, pleasure and amusement as the real object of life? We had to do a job of work so as to earn the means of enjoying ourselves when it was done; but that enjoyment was what we really lived for—not for the service to the common good that we gave through our work. And why did we shirk, as undoubtedly we did, our share of the burden of maintaining international order? Was it not once more our unwillingness for the discipline and discomfort of military training? Of course this was not the only reason; but I am sure it played its part. A rather sentimentalized religious faith combined with a rather aimless love of comfort, to make us hope for the blessings of peace without shouldering our share of its burden. Especially have we been unwilling to ask our neighbours or our children for hard or difficult service. Even when we have accepted high standards for ourselves, we have hesitated to call others to live by them. But this is sheer arrogance masquerading as kindness. You cannot insult a man more atrociously than by offering him a lower standard than your own. We must recover faith—virile faith—in God, and dedication—costly dedication—to His service, if we are not to slip back into the rather listless and complacent state from which the challenge of the war has roused us.

"All very well," perhaps you say; "but how am I to follow God's purpose in my life? And am I to believe that His purpose for me is the monotonous drudgery which is demanded of so many folk to-day?" Here we come to the second group of considerations. Because we have neglected God, we have also neglected His law. We have forgotten that we are His creatures equally with the other animals and with the earth itself. Leaving God out of account, we have found ourselves able to utilize all natural resources for our purposes and have regarded ourselves as lords of creation. So we have turned the bounty of nature to the satisfaction of our greed, with the result that the whole economic system is now upside down. It is clear that, in the natural order of things, God's order, the object of all industry is the supply of men's wants; in the language of the economist, the consumer is the person whose interest should be supreme in determining the whole process; for his sake goods are produced; and finance comes in as the servant of production. But in our world, goods are produced, not primarily to satisfy the consumer, but to enrich the producer. The profit-motive predominates over the service-motive; and this inversion of all that is right is gone so far, that now finance controls production instead of production controlling finance, and the consumer, for whose benefit alone production really goes on at all, becomes no more than an indispensable condition of successful business enterprise.

Now the predominance of the profit-motive is itself a source of war. When I come to speak about international and social justice, I shall argue that the industrial system familiar to us before the war broke out was itself a predisposing cause of war. Also it stood condemned as ineffective in its function, by the fact of widespread unemployment. It must be re-modelled. But if that is done under pressure of competing class-interests, the remedy may be worse than the disease. We must try to find God's way of ordering our life and follow that. " Seek ye first the Kingdom of God and His justice, and all these things "— food, clothing, economic good as a whole—" shall be added unto you."

II

God and Freedom

We constantly remind ourselves that this is a war between freedom and tyranny. That is absolutely true, and cannot be too prominent in our minds. If the Nazis win there will be no freedom left in Europe for many a year to come—no freedom of conscience, for the young people will be trained to believe that the Leader is always right; no freedom of speech, for criticism of the Leader and his subordinates is forbidden; no freedom of thought, for if men may not express their thoughts their minds will atrophy; no freedom of spirit, for allegiance to the State will be inculcated as the only way of serving God.

Against this repudiation of freedom we are fighting. But let us remember that in the last twenty years we have seen nations deliberately reject freedom, believing it to be a source of disunion, a hindrance to fellowship, and a cause of degeneration. When great multitudes of people adopt an idea it may be more false than true, but it is unlikely to be simply and solely false. What have these people seen in free institutions which has led them to repudiate freedom for themselves and try to spread that repudiation through the world as a kind of new gospel? Let us try to draw the picture which they have had before their minds. It is a picture of society where everyone claims the right to do what seems good to him; where each individual, each family, above all each economic class, puts self-interest before all other considerations; where, at times of political elections, candidates compete in offering to different sections of the constituency the satisfaction of their desires; where those politicians gain power and determine policy who are most skilful in offering attractive baits to voters. In other words, it is a society where every man uses his freedom to advance his own interest. In contrast with this, is set the vision of a society where all are swept into the service of the common purpose by suppression of individual desires and the enlistment of each in the enterprise of all.

I am not now concerned with the methods by which, in fact, the intense unification of Germany has been carried out—the Gestapo, Concentration Camps and the like. I am concerned with the German picture of the democratic nations. Is there any real truth in it? Of course it is not wholly true. The unity of our people in the war effort of this moment would be impossible if that picture were wholly true. But when we look back to the days of peace, do we not recall many features in our national life which bear a closer resemblance to this German caricature than we like? And if we have to admit this, must we not go on to ask how far freedom is necessarily accompanied by these bad results, and what we can do to avoid them?

Freedom is not a perfectly simple idea. At first, we mostly understand it as being allowed to do what we choose, and that is certainly part of it. But whether this will, in fact, lead to our happiness, depends on our capacity — moral and intellectual — to choose wisely. If at any moment our desires are thwarted, that, as far as it goes, is disagreeable and makes us to that extent less happy; but if the desire is for something unwholesome, the satisfaction of it may make us a great deal more unhappy. The fact is, that along with all our momentary desires we have some steady purpose in life, and fulfilment of this has much more to do with happiness than has the satisfaction or non-satisfaction of desires. For example, we very quickly learn to make physical health, or keeping fit, a part of our steady purpose; it may involve refusing to eat some kinds of food which would give us a great deal of momentary pleasure. If that is so, our happiness depends on the self-control which enables us to refuse the unwholesome delicacy. In other words, the freedom that matters is not freedom to satisfy our momentary desires, but freedom to fulfil our steady and constant purpose. The main business of education is to strengthen our capacity to form and follow an adequate purpose throughout life.

How do we form that purpose? If we are left to ourselves, we build it up by putting together the things that matter most to us and so arranging life as to secure a reasonable amount of these. Each man's selection will vary according to his gifts, temperament and interests. But for every one they will include a home of sufficient comfort and congenial companionship. These objects will lead a man to develop his gregarious instincts—his impulses towards common feeling and generosity—to a considerable extent. Also he will readily accept so much regulation of his life by law as obtains for him security through the same regulation of other people's lives. Such a man may be a law-abiding, useful citizen and an agreeable member of his own society. But in the end, his own happiness, comfort and convenience are the decisive factors in directing his life and in moulding his estimate of social or national policy. His first, and probably last, question concerning any proposal, personal or public, will be: How does this affect me and my family or friends? Other questions may come in between; but that is likely to come both first and last, and the answer to it almost alone decides his attitude.

If my freedom means chiefly my being left to do what I must choose, it must chiefly express itself in this way. And a society based on that kind of freedom alone will be a welter of competing selfishness, held together in some kind of order because chaos means misery for all; but the order of that society may be broken up by any group which at any time has both desire and power to gain some advantage by an upheaval. This is the freedom which expresses itself in strikes and lock-outs, and other features of a democratic system which have led the totalitarian countries to turn away from freedom as from a radically false principle of life.

It cannot be denied that a great part of the inspiration of democracy has come from this self-assertive type of freedom. It has advanced by attack upon privilege and affirmation of rights. Mazzini constantly urged that it should be based rather upon duties than upon rights; but it is at best doubtful whether, in this respect, he was able to exert any powerful influence. We have to recognize that democracy, as we have known it, displays some of the characteristics for which the totalitarian States denounce it; and we must also recognize that so long as men base their attachment to freedom on the opportunity which it brings to follow their own choice or purpose, so long will freedom and democracy deserve at least some measure of that denunciation.

But there is an older tradition of freedom than that which has been so prominent since the time of the French Revolution; its authentic formulation is: " We must obey God rather than men." The real reason why the State must not presume to dictate to me my manner of life and thought is not that I am myself, but that I am a child of God. Historically the first claim to liberty successfully asserted against the modern State was the claim to worship God according to conscience. It is this which makes the Dutch Protestants, who rose against Philip II of Spain, the true pioneers of European liberty; and in our own country the successful assertion of the same claim by groups attached to different beliefs in a series of political upheavals was the well-spring of English liberty as we know it to-day. Often these pioneers had little understanding of what they were doing and set no store at all by liberty as a principle. But they heard in their consciences what they believed to be the voice of God; and by the constancy of their obedience to that voice they won the right to freedom of conscience for themselves and for us.

Freedom of conscience—that is the sacred thing: not freedom to do what I choose or to fulfil my own purpose, but freedom to do what I ought, and to fulfil God's purpose for me. Of course the political forms which guarantee this freedom of conscience open the way also to the freedom of self-assertion; and this latter always follows the other like a dark shadow.

In the pressures of the modern world the freedom of man in his human right alone cannot stand; nor does it deserve to stand. It is a sham and a usurpation. It is a sham because it poses as real freedom when, in fact, it is nothing of the kind. "Doing what I like" is what St. Paul accurately describes as "the body of this death"; for my likes and dislikes are not free; they are fixed by my heredity, training and circumstance. As I pursue my self-chosen way, I come, inevitably, into collision with others pursuing theirs, and in the conflict both lose all satisfaction. If you watch the characters in Shakespeare—most penetrating reader of the hearts of men—you will find that only his villains assert their power to control their own lives—men like Edmund in *King Lear* or Iago in *Othello*. So far as I am not coerced by others, I have a formal kind of freedom, for my self is the origin of my conduct; but there is no substance in that freedom, for from my self there is no escape.

This self-centred freedom—" I am the master of my fate "—is a snare to the individual and a menace to society. For the individual supposes himself free because he is "tied and bound by the chain of his sins"; and the society is called free because its members are unhindered in destroying it if they will. Once again—the expression of this liberty is in strikes and lock-outs, which are the result of the free self-assertion of one group against another group to the detriment of society as a whole, and probably also of both the groups concerned.

But if I claim freedom over against the State because I am a child of God and must obey Him rather than men, there is no risk (except so far as I delude myself) that I shall use this freedom to pursue my own advantage to the detriment of either my neighbour or society as a whole. For God loves all His children, and that divine purpose which I claim liberty to serve includes the welfare of them all. This freedom is indeed indestructible by the earthly State, except through the extermination of all who assert it; but it is no enemy to a State which aims at establishing justice between its members, for in pursuit of that aim the State will find its God-fearing citizens actively co-operating.

Every day it becomes clearer that the root of the main political problems of to-day is religious—the presence or absence of faith in God. If this world is the creation of God who is the Father of all men and has made Himself known in Jesus Christ, then each man, because he is a child of God, has a dignity higher than any earthly title and a value independent of any State. That is his claim to freedom, and the claim carries with it the security against its own abuse; for it is freedom to serve God. Samuel Taylor Coleridge was profoundly right when he defined man's true freedom as "the power of the human being to maintain the obedience, which God through the conscience has commanded, against all the might of nature".[1]

So our service of freedom in these days requires of us two things; first, that we should save it from the threat which hangs over it, by driving back and destroying the Nazi tyranny; but also see to it that our freedom is rooted in that faith in God which alone can nurture it as a vigorous and healthy plant. We must return to God, and learn again, by experiment and experience, how true it is that His service

[1] *The Friend*, Vol. I, p. 143.

is perfect freedom, and that the only true freedom is His service. How we may do it, we shall consider next week. But our present duty is to secure the freedom which we defend not only from external attack but from internal decay. If the aim of the last war was to make the world safe for democracy and freedom, our aim in this war must be to make freedom and democracy safe for the world. It is my conviction that only a freedom rooted in faith is able to survive, or deserves to survive. Man must learn again that he is not the lord of creation but himself a creature, and, acknowledging the gift of freedom, also confess to the Creator " Our wills are ours to make them Thine ".

III

Prayer and its answer

What I have said in the two former talks may be summed up in this way: the war is itself a call to us to return to God, to become aware of Him as the supreme reality, and to dedicate ourselves to Him both individually and as a nation. Now the question arises for everyone, How can I take my part in this?

I am disposed to begin by making what many people will feel to be a quite outrageous statement. This world can be saved from political chaos and collapse by one thing only, and that is worship. As I said, it sounds outrageous. How in the world can we solve the problems of international rivalries and social inequalities by all going to church? And how like a parson to suggest it! It is just an instance of grinding his own axe; and so far as it has any effect at all it can only be what Karl Marx called religion—dope for the masses.

That is a perfectly natural and wholesome reaction. And let us clear up a few points at once. Those of us who are parsons are tempted to attach excessive importance to people's use of our ministrations; and some of us yield to the temptation. I remember hearing one of the great religious teachers of our time, Father Herbert Kelly, say to a group of men preparing for ordination, "Don't make the mistake of trying to give all your people religion; most of them have not much time for religion; what they need is faith." But of course that same teacher has often told us that faith can only be real if it is exercised and expressed. You express whatever faith you have already got by your action, especially at critical moments; but you get more faith chiefly by worship.

I do not suppose that anyone is going to say again, "It does not matter what a man believes." It obviously matters a great deal to all of us what the Nazis believe. They believe it with great fervour; and we are not going to extirpate their belief by a mild haze of cautiously held opinions. If when a man says

"I believe in God" what he really means is "I suppose there is some sort of God somewhere", it is quite unimportant whether he holds that opinion or its opposite. But the opening words of the Creed do not mean that; they mean "I put my trust in God". Every man who says that with reality is at once expressing a faith which he already holds, and reminding himself how very feeble a thing it is; for unless he is a perfect saint he does not completely put his trust in God, but knows that he cannot live as he hopes to live till he trusts God more. He joins in the affirmation of the Church; but for himself it is chiefly an aspiration towards something not yet actual.

How is he to make it actual? If we are to put the world to rights, we must first put ourselves right. We must trust God more than we do. But you cannot trust anyone to order. Trust, which is always on the way to being love, must be spontaneous or non-existent. It grows of itself within our hearts as we come to appreciate the character and wisdom of someone whose record we know; and it grows most surely when we come to know personally in actual companionship someone who, the more we know him, inspires in us more trust and confidence in his character and wisdom.

Trust in God grows in just the same way. But because He is God, companionship with Him is worship. Just consider what are the component parts of worship as we find them in a familiar form of service

like the morning and evening services in the Prayer
Book. We come into the presence of the Holy God,
and exactly in proportion to our appreciation of His
holiness we feel unworthy to be there, and express
this in our confession of sin. Then after hearing the
declaration of the pardon which His love assures to
us, we join in praise of His goodness in the Psalms,
which rise out of every kind of human joy, sorrow,
perplexity, anxiety and doubt. Assured of His goodness despite all that our experience may contain, we
open our minds to receive something more of His
truth. In the phrase used just now, we study His
record. As a result we affirm our faith in the Creed
which should always be a confession of the trust we
already have in God and an aspiration towards the
deeper trust which we need. Then, in that trust, we
bring our needs before Him in prayer for ourselves,
for our nation, for our Church, for all who are in
need.

Of course, if all you do in church is to sit, stand
and kneel when others do, while someone else says
things to which you attend, to see where he has got
to as your mind returns from "going to and fro in
the earth and walking up and down in it", you are
not doing yourself much good and are doing the rest
of the congregation a good deal of harm by diluting
the atmosphere of devotion. In that case you are not
worshipping at all. But if you are entering into it,
if you are really worshipping at all, then you are doing

just what is most needed to enable you to take your part in bringing in the new world for which we hope. For to worship is to quicken the conscience by the holiness of God, to feed the mind with the truth of God, to purge the imagination by the beauty of God, to open the heart to the love of God, to devote the will to the purpose of God. All this is gathered up in that emotion which most cleanses us from selfishness because it is the most selfless of all emotions—adoration.

We want to reach the stage when we naturally and spontaneously act by trust in God. But we have not reached it; at least, I have not and I do not suppose you have. And that being so, it is mere humbug to say that we will serve God by our conduct but cannot find time for prayer and worship. If that is all we do, we shall serve Him just as much as we have been doing—which is what has brought the world to the mess it is now in. We must have our times for companionship with God, the companionship which, because He is God, is worship, the companionship which causes our trust in Him and our love for Him to grow.

Now prayer, as we usually understand the word— that is to say, asking God for benefits of various kinds —is one part of worship, and is in place only in that setting. That is why the first clause in the model prayer is "Hallowed be Thy Name". By the way, how often do you pray that? Of course you say it over and over again, if you pray at all. But how often do you pray it? You cannot pray it unless you want it at least a little. Do you care at all whether God is honoured and reverenced "in earth as in heaven"? You cannot offer a truly Christian prayer for daily bread or for forgiveness unless you have prayed for God's honour and glory: for Christ Himself put this first of all petitions.

So it is as true worshippers, or at any rate as would-be true worshippers, that we make our requests. That of itself will settle the kind of things we ask for and the spirit in which we ask for them. There is, indeed, no reason why we should hesitate to bring before our Father any innocent desire that we have. He loves us and desires our happiness. But He knows that our real happiness depends much more on our characters than on the satisfaction of our particular desires; and He is the Father of the whole human family who will not grant the requests of some of His children in ways that would injure others. Therefore we must not expect that He will answer any selfish prayers of ours in the form in which we present them.

We pray because the realization that God is the source of all good may be the condition to be fulfilled before some gift will be a real blessing. If the good thing came without our realizing its source, the result might be to fix us in forgetfulness of God; and then it would have brought injury to us, not benefit. But as we remember Him as the source of all good, we

31

remember also who and what He is, and what kind of thing is good in His sight. So, though we bring Him all our needs and hopes, we also recognize that what we should choose may not be best at all, and check our desires by the overruling petition, "Not my will, but Thine be done."

Our prayers for ourselves are usually at first for success, for health, for happiness, or for some form of strength which we know we lack. The chief thing to remember about prayers for success is that we can only ask God for this with reason so far as we believe our plan to be part of His. As we pray for increase of strength or virtue, let us remember that the answer is likely to take the form of opportunity to exercise it, like the lady who prayed for patience and was provided with an ill-tempered cook. As our prayers are deepened we more and more let self-dedication take the place of petition for ourselves. We learn to put ourselves in God's hands for Him to do with us what He will; and so we become more sensitive to the prompting of His Spirit. Some people call this listening to God; that is a good phrase so long as it does not suggest that we expect precise messages giving particular directions. Such messages may come and we should be ready for them; but they are rare. More often we hear no special message, but find when the time comes that we do or say the right thing because our impulses and judgment are under the influence of God in whose hands we have placed our lives. We should in that way commit ourselves to God at the beginning of each day, thinking as we do so of the experiences which we expect that day to bring.

At a time like this we think more of prayer for our friends than for ourselves. What shall we pray for them—for our friends in the Navy, Army or Air Force, for example? Shall we pray that God will bring them safely home? Yes, certainly—but not chiefly. We know that they in their best moments do not put safety first. No; our first prayer must be that God will keep them brave and steadfast, loyal to Him, to country and to comrades. If that loyalty means death, we would not have them kept from death at the cost of disloyalty. After all, death is worse for the friends who still live than for those who die out of loyalty. In life and in death we are in our Father's keeping, and nothing in life or death is really bad except the selfishness which comes out as cruelty in peace or as cowardice in war.

How are such prayers answered? Does God deflect bullets in the air or vary the changes of the weather? Of course He could. But we have no right to expect miracles. The fixed course of nature is the necessary framework for our moral and spiritual life, and it would be bad for us if it were frequently modified to suit our convenience. Yet there are some points to remember here. First, we still know very little about the control which spirit can exercise over matter, and the spiritual energy of fervent prayer may be a factor in determining some physical occurrences. Secondly, God's view of the world is not like ours along one line from past through present to an unknown future; it is eternal knowledge, and much which to us appears coincidence may be a connexion planned by Him. Thirdly and above all, the usual sphere of His operation is in the hearts and minds of men. I have seen it said that the deliverance at Dunkirk may have been an answer to prayer but was more certainly due to the devotion, enterprise, courage and discipline of Navy, Mercantile Marine, Army and Air Force. Certainly it was due to these, but where do these come from? Those who are accustomed to pray to the "Lord of all power and might" who is "the author and giver of all good things" will not draw any contrast there. All honour to the heroic men through whom that deliverance was wrought; and thanks be to God who inspired and sustained them in their endurance and achievement.

Prayer, as we learn more of it, becomes more and more the expression of our trust in God for all for whom we pray, ourselves included. Many people just now are puzzled by the quite clear teaching of Christ that we should pray for our enemies. As far as I can judge from what they say about this, the whole difficulty arises from the supposition that if we pray for anyone we must ask God to give him what he wishes to receive. But whether we pray for friends or for enemies our chief prayer must be that in and among them God's Name may be hallowed, His Kingdom come and His Will be done; and any particular benefit for which we ask is brought in as part of the fulfilment of that fundamental request. If those first petitions of the Lord's Prayer were fulfilled in Germany to-day, the war could end to-morrow, for it would involve the renunciation of the whole Nazi philosophy and the aggression which it has inspired.

Those who pray as Christ taught us to pray are never praying against each other; for they do not pray that their own will may be done, but God's, which they know to be better than their own for themselves and for all men. Such prayer is the outward reach of the spirit of worship. It is the dedication of ourselves, our loved ones and all for whom we pray to the Father whose wisdom and love are greater than our own.

IV

International Justice

In the two previous talks I have spoken about the definitely religious subjects—faith and prayer. Now we pass to the expression of faith in practical obedience. To some people the subjects which I shall deal with seem to fall outside the sphere of religion altogether; and it is true that detailed application always calls for knowledge of facts and technical competence as well as for the right spirit. But the principles of conduct in all departments of life belong to the sphere of religion; for God is supreme over all life and at all points we must obey Him if we have faith in Him; and this obedience must in the new world-order take the form of an endeavour to establish international and social justice.

The proposition that we must aim at International Justice in the post-war settlement will not be disputed in any quarter. But there are some quarters in which this is taken to mean simply either punishment of Germany or equal treatment of Germany, and some in which it is developed into elaborate schemes which ignore many essential factors in the situation. If we are to think clearly about this immense subject we must keep some distinctions carefully in mind. The first is the distinction between the immediate settlement after the war and the settlement which is intended to last for an indefinite period. There must in any case be first an armistice and later the permanent peace; I hope that besides the armistice there may be an interim settlement while preparations are made for reaching the terms of the permanent peace. Why this seems desirable I will explain in a moment.

Secondly, there is the distinction familiar to moral philosophers between Corrective Justice and Distributive Justice, where the former is concerned with the proper treatment of someone who has committed an injury and readjustment of the situation which the injurious action has vitiated, and the latter—Distributive Justice—is concerned with establishing fair relations between various parties without reference to any question of injury or wrong in the past. Again, there are three different aspects of Corrective Justice in its penal aspects—the justice administered in a criminal court—namely Retributive (so-called), Deterrent, and Reformative; that is to say, the wrong-doer must get his deserts, the crime must be shown up as not worth while, and the criminal must be put in the way of becoming again a useful citizen.

It is commonly laid down as a principle of justice that no man should be judge in his own cause; and I believe that one of the chief necessities, if justice is to be established and with it a hope of peace, is that all nations should forgo the right to judge their own cause. Thus, to take a concrete illustration, Sir Austen Chamberlain said to me shortly before he died that he would like to make the League of Nations the arbiter of the Locarno Treaty, whereas by the terms of the treaty each nation signing it retained the right to determine whether or not a situation had arisen which called for a fulfilment of obligations under the treaty. That illustrates the goal to which we must move. But war is in its very nature a repudiation of legal or judicial methods, and it would not be possible to leave to any tribunal the drawing up of the terms of an armistice. If we win the war—and of course all talk about our hope of a new world assumes that we mean to win the war and shall win it—we must ourselves settle the terms of the Armistice. The primary consideration here is that the enemy be effectively hindered from renewing hostilities. The Armistice of 1918 admirably illustrates what is required; but to put beyond dispute the fact of Germany's defeat, this might well have been followed by a march across Germany and a temporary occupation of Berlin.

After the Armistice will come the need for some speedy settlement on the basis of which trade may start again and the economic life of the nations may begin to be restored. In making this settlement all the nations defeated or occupied by Germany should have a voice, with neutrals, if by then there are any, as assessors. We must be prepared for a great financial crisis in Germany; for the money in circulation depends on the moral credit of the Nazi Government and on its power to compel acceptance of its currency at face value. When the Nazi regime falls, it may be that no alternative Government will be able quickly to assume that burden of public confidence, so that the money in circulation may suddenly be valueless; then we shall be obliged to supply as best we can a basis for German credit, so that some semblance of ordered life may be preserved.

It is most desirable to make an *interim* settlement

for two reasons: first, it will give time for passions to cool and a dispassionate judgment to be formed; in a period of five years men would be able to see what are the real problems needing solution. Secondly, such an interval gives opportunity for preparation both in collection of facts and in consultation, so that the general peace conference may meet with the best hope of success.

This interim settlement should be in part penal. It provides the moment for corrective justice. If there is no penal element in this truce, the result must be a condonation of the wrong that Germany has done to Europe. Three times in three-quarters of a century a Prussianized Germany has caused devastation and misery by carefully planned aggression. It must be made clear to all German people that such aggression brings calamity to the aggressor as well as to his victims. This is required by justice and is, I think, a necessary preliminary to the re-education of the German mind vitiated by years of Nazi propaganda. But the penal element of the truce should be such as to touch the national and political rather than the personal and economic life of the people; only so will it be relevant. One suggestion which deserves careful consideration is that the ancient German nations should be reconstituted as they were before the rise of Bismarck. The revival of the States suppressed by him for the aggrandizement of Prussia would of itself end the dominance of Prussia over Germany. These

States should for a time be garrisoned by the Allies; but it must always be understood that, before the final settlement is made, they shall be free to come together in any way that they themselves choose to make again a united Germany. If that is not secured, the passion for unity will again break out in rebellion against the whole European settlement.

I shall probably be told that to advocate any penal action is contrary to the Christian principle of free forgiveness; but here two considerations must be borne in mind: first, Christianity recognizes that forgiveness, to be real, must be costly. The Redeemer of the world took the cost upon Himself upon the Cross. Some Christian saints have been able to come near to that manifestation of divine love. But, secondly, no nation has ever been Christian in a degree that makes that possible, and where it is not possible, infliction of a just penalty is nearer to Christian righteousness than such action as seems to condone the wrong.[1]

While then the terms of this preliminary settlement or truce should contain elements designed to express and bring home to Germany the moral condemnation which she has earned, yet this penal quality should belong only to the truce and not to the permanent settlement. When we reach that stage all thought of corrective justice must be eliminated. There must be no new generation growing up under the embitter-

[1] See Note 1 on p. 44.

ing conditions of a penal peace. Indeed when we consider how the generations pass, it is evident that no penal element in a peace-treaty can be both permanent and just; as the years pass, it will become increasingly an oppression and an injustice, for it presses upon citizens not guilty of the crime. The permanent settlement must aim at Distributive Justice, all nations, including Germany, taking part on equal terms in the negotiations, and all having equal claim to consideration and their fair share in organizing the common life for the common good.

Why was the League of Nations only partially successful in this enterprise? Is it not clear that it attempted a compromise where no compromise is possible? It relied upon sanctions, yet left the essential sovereignty of the national States untouched. It did in some ways profoundly modify that sovereignty; but at the crucial point of decision, whether or not economic or military sanctions should be imposed, it left the several States sovereign. By including sanctions the Covenant undermined the purely moral authority of the Council and Assembly of the League, for attention was diverted from this, which might otherwise carry much weight, to the question whether force was to be applied. By leaving the Sovereign States to decide upon the application of sanctions, it made that application uncertain and precarious; indeed, experience showed that the several States were not prepared to resort to force unless their own vital interests were affected, and did not regard the maintenance of international law as one of those vital interests.

There is obviously no middle way between International Anarchy (such as has existed since the break up of the Roman Empire and even avowedly since A.D. 1500) and some form of Federation. But the actual Federation of Europe is a colossal task. We must keep it before us as our goal; but if we attempt to rush it, any measure of temporary success will be wiped out in the ensuing set-back. What then can we do? First our own and other nations can commit themselves negatively if not positively; they can undertake after peace is restored never to use their armed forces except either to repel an attack actually delivered or else in conformity with the international authority. Further, it may be possible to equip that authority with an efficient Air Force and to abolish all other military aviation; if this involves an international control of all aviation whatsoever, let it be so.[1]

But the new unity must be constructed, not out of paper schemes, but out of actual co-operation. Behind all problems of international friction is the economic condition of the world. Science has enabled us to produce wealth in wholly unexampled abundance; but our organization of life is based on the expectation of expanding markets to absorb expanding production;

[1] See Note 2 on p. 45.

and the markets do not any longer expand in that degree. So it happens that the ease with which we produce becomes a reason for not producing at all, because the markets are glutted, though human need is not satisfied. Under existing conditions we can only solve the paradox of poverty in the midst of plenty by abolishing the plenty!

I believe that the way of hope, because it is the way of mutual service, is to call all nations to the co-operative enterprise of making the wealth now so easily produced available for the needs of all peoples, or, to put it otherwise, the raising of the standard of life for the masses of the people in all nations by making available to them the wealth of the world. In pursuing that aim of general human service we shall be brought into increasingly close association and the federal union which we hope for will rather grow than be made or imposed. We shall, for example, deal in this way with the vexed question of access to raw materials far better than by trying to distribute control of them among the nations or by an attempt to pool sovereignty at the very outset. And commerce must become avowedly an exchange of goods for mutual advantage, in which all search for what is called a favourable trade balance is repudiated; the pursuit by every nation of a favourable trade balance is inevitably a source of conflict; for if the balance is favourable to one it must be unfavourable to another.

Now for any such policy to have success two things

will be needed: a change in the social and economic order of many countries, including our own, and a restriction of the acquisitive impulse which has in the past been at once a mainspring of economic progress and a source of disunion. We must surrender much of national pride and something of national responsibility. The more fortunate sections of our country, probably including some grades of labour, must be ready to accept a reduced standard of living, so that the good things of the earth may be more equitably shared both between the nations and within the nations.

When we consider what is the price that we must pay for securing approximate international justice and a fair hope of peace, we can see that all our spiritual resources will be called on to the uttermost if we are worthily to play our part. There must be no relaxation after this war; but as by sacrifice and fortitude we shall win the war, so by sacrifice and magnanimity we must establish true peace.

NOTE I

It is a misrepresentation of the Gospel to say that it contains an offer of " free forgiveness ", because this is so easily interpreted as an unconditional offer of forgiveness, and this the Gospel does not contain. Its offer of forgiveness is conditional, though when the condition is fulfilled the forgiveness is freely given.

What is the condition? The usual answer is " repentance "; and this answer is right, so far as it goes, if the word carries its whole New Testament sense. This is nothing less than the change of heart which leads us to take God's view of the world instead of our own; it is the reversal of our Original Sin. And this is not in our power. I cannot repent to order any more than I can love or trust to order.

But there is another condition. The antagonism of holiness—the " wrath of God "—against evil must be expressed; there must be no condonation of evil. This condition is fulfilled in the Cross. For the Cross is what man's sin (selfishness) does to God; and God accepts it. But when the word of pardon is accompanied by that manifestation of what the injury really was and is, no one can think of condonation.

It is only when forgiveness is accompanied or preceded by such agony that it is altogether right. That is why St. Paul says that the Cross enables God to be just while He forgives, to forgive while remaining just.

No man can quite reach that height. No nation can come near it, nor ever will be able to do so while History lasts. For History is the record of man's entanglement in sin; and though in the final consummation sin will be done away, that consummation lies beyond the historical process. So we have not got to consider what perfectly righteous England might achieve, but what is the best that sinful England may hope to do.

NOTE 2

Those who wish to study a well thought out scheme of Federation may be recommended to read Sir William Beveridge's pamphlet *Peace by Federation* published by the Federal Union.

v

Social Justice

There has never yet been a state of society in which perfect justice was established. This could only be done if all citizens completely obeyed the command "Thou shalt love thy neighbour as thyself". Of course that has never happened; indeed it is unlikely that any single individual, except our Lord Himself, ever obeyed that commandment perfectly. We are all of us born self-centred; that is our Original Sin. We estimate the value and importance of things by the way in which they affect ourselves. Some by education, and more deeply by conversion, are enabled to escape from a great deal of this entanglement of self-interest; but all of us are involved in it more or less. Our task as Churchmen is to submit ourselves to the power which can effect our deliverance and to direct other people to it; our task as Christian citizens is to take our share in so moulding society that the nearest practicable approximation to justice is actually established.

If we approach the matter as Christians, we shall be careful to understand this in terms of personal life rather than of purely economic wealth; from this standpoint the most serious inequality to-day is found in the matter of educational opportunity. We have made great strides in this field during the present century: the position is entirely different from what it was in 1900. When the State began to interest itself in education, in the middle of the nineteenth century, it almost inevitably worked by the principle of an irreducible minimum—a point to which all children must be brought. At the outset, it was impossible to aim at more. But this had deplorable results, including the notorious half-time system, and a provision under which children who reached the required standards could leave school a year before the general school-leaving age. In other words, if a child was clever enough to profit by remaining at school, it was allowed to leave early; if it was too stupid to gain much from it, it had to stay there for the full period.

Moreover, what was envisaged was schooling rather than education. The first board schools, which, as Charles Masterman said, "proclaimed, by the very audacity of their ferocious ugliness, the advantages of State-given education", were no more than vast boxes of class-rooms. There was no corporate life of the school, and no attempt to make its architecture the expression of a communal life. The entire conception was purely individualistic: the children were taught in droves because it was too expensive to teach them separately. The fact that the school itself can and should be the great educator of its pupils, apart from

47

all instruction given by teachers, was almost completely ignored.

A vast change has come since 1900, and especially since 1920. But we are still far from that measure of equality in educational opportunity which can be provided in spite of the inevitable differences in the cultural quality of homes and families. Those differences, indeed, cannot be removed unless (as Plato advocated, partly with this object) the family is abolished and children are brought up in State institutions. These differences in home training are not chiefly a matter of social class or of income, though poverty is a dire hindrance to culture. There are plenty of aristocratic and of wealthy homes in which the children very seldom hear any intelligent conversation; and there are plenty of poor and of working-class homes where they hear a great deal; and the most influential of all educational factors is the conversation in a child's home.

These differences in home influence will persist. But the opportunities provided outside the home should be as far as possible the same for all. Of course this does not mean that everyone is to be taught the same things. That would be most unfair, for the subjects selected would suit some and not others. There must be the greatest possible variety, and the aim must be the fullest possible development of each according to his or her talent. We have abandoned the principle of the irreducible minimum. We must deliberately

48

adopt that of the maximum attainable.

The vital point is this. The community of young people is itself the great educator; and care must be taken that all young people up to the age of eighteen are members of such a community or fellowship, enjoying its support and braced by consciousness of responsibility for its tradition and welfare. This community need not be a school if by that we mean a place of book-learning; but it must be a place of training for citizenship by the actual experience and practice of life in a community. The newly launched Youth Movement may do great things here if it is conceived on lines sufficiently bold and untraditional.

But more potent than school, or even than home, as a moral influence, is the whole structure of society, and especially its economic structure. This fixes for all their place in the general scheme; and the way in which they gain and keep that place of necessity determines a great deal of their conduct and profoundly influences their outlook upon life. Can it be said that the social and economic system with which we have been familiar, expresses and inculcates a view of human life akin to Christianity? The salient feature of it, when judged from this standpoint, is the fact of unemployment on a large scale. In the middle of last summer—1940—the expert correspondent of *The Times*, commenting on the fact that the figure for unemployment was then three-quarters of a million, said that this was probably near the minimum, even

though millions of young men are in the Forces and
we are making our maximum effort. If that is so, it
is a sign that our system, as we have known it, is
inadequate to our needs. It is clearly demanded by
social justice that we should gain for the mass of the
people deliverance from this nightmare of insecurity.

There is another equally serious charge to be laid
against it: it contains the seeds of war, because it
relies so largely on the profit-motive, with which love
of power is closely bound up. No doubt it is not the
economic system itself so much as policies associated
with it which tend towards conflict. But the tendency
is there. The Directors of Companies are elected by
shareholders, whose interest in the company is that it
should pay the best possible dividends. This was
always open to objection on moral grounds, but at least
it supplied a useful stimulus to production in a period
when the market was capable of indefinite expansion.
But this is no longer true. The market to-day does
not expand in such a way as to keep pace with the
increased power of production. Consequently there is
competition for the limited market; and as the well-
being of whole nations depends on that competition,
we have here an occasion of international conflict. It
may never reach the point of open war. There are
very few businesses that profit by war, and far the
majority of industrialists desire peace. But they also
desire what tends to destroy peace, and thus the working of the system has an inherent tendency towards

international rivalry, jealousy and conflict.

The root of the trouble is that we have deserted the natural order. In the nature of things the object of producing goods is that human needs may be satisfied; in economic terms, production exists for the sake of the consumer. Consequently, the production of food should be regulated with a view to satisfying the hunger of men—not with a view to the profits of the producers. Of course they cannot work at a loss; that leads to bankruptcy and cessation of the whole process. But the organization could be so devised as to express and secure the predominant interest of the consumer.

Now the consumer is the general public. Every man is a consumer, whether he is also a producer or not; that is why idleness and theft are morally indistinguishable. The idle man (however much he legally possesses) is consuming without producing; he enjoys what he does not earn. As Paulsen remarked: "'If any will not work neither let him eat' is only another way of saying 'Thou shalt not steal'." But if there is an obligation upon every man to contribute something, spiritual, intellectual or material, to the common stock on which he draws to keep himself alive, it is also true that it is for the satisfaction of his needs and those of his fellows that the whole process of industry exists.

It is easy to infer from this that some form of Communism or State Socialism is the ideal system. But these ignore the fact that a man is still a human being in his activity as a producer and not only as a consumer; he ought to have free play for his personality, as far as may be, in the act of production—and this is the root-truth of individualistic capitalism. Our task must be to do justice as far as possible to the truth of capitalism, as well as to the truth of socialism.

To this end the State, as the representative of the whole community and, therefore, of the consumer, must undertake the planning of our economic life, taking care, as far as may be, that all essential needs are met, and that there is no glutting of the market so that stoppage occurs in that process of production whereby most men earn their livelihood.

There may be some industries which are best conducted by management directly responsible to the State, as the Post Office is. But this should probably be rare and confined to services indispensable to the whole community. For State management involves bureaucracy, and this easily becomes as stifling to free personality as grinding competition. We do not want one cast-iron system but the fullest attainable combination of order or planning with freedom or personal initiative.

I start with the economic legislation of the Bible. The principle of the Divine Law as there set out for economics is to allow the maximum personal freedom compatible with the prevention of all exploitation either of the land by any person or group, or of one person or group by another. Thus in the Law of

Moses purchase of land in perpetuity is forbidden, for the land belongs to God and is granted by Him to His people for their use. Now it is the Common Law of England at this moment that all the land of England belongs to the King as representing the whole community and the divinely constituted authority within it. And so-called landowners hold the use of the land but not absolute dominion over it. They can therefore be restrained from a use or development of the land which might be profitable to them but detrimental to the public interest, and this should be done much more than it is. Town-planning legislation, for example, is still in its infancy, and the instalments we have yet had are cautious or timid as you please, but certainly not bold. It must, however, be recognized that the rural landlord discharges many social functions, and ownership of agricultural land, subject to consideration of the public welfare, should not be subject to the same restrictions as ownership of industrial stocks and shares; moreover, as family tradition is in this field a valuable social asset I should personally urge the total exemption of all agricultural land from death duties.[1]

The social function of the urban landlord is less evident; and the social function of the ordinary shareholder as such simply does not exist. The ancient Law of Jubilee, whereby once in fifty years the original equal distribution of land was to be re-

[1] See Note 1 on p. 57.

stored, can therefore be applied more directly to these. It can be done in any one of three ways or by a combination of these: shares may take the form of debentures and be repayable at a certain date; or invested capital after bearing interest for a number of years may lose a proportion of its value each year till it is extinguished; or the inheritance of it may be curtailed by drastic death duties. In one way or another it should be secured that no one by investing capital alone can become possessed of a permanent and saleable right to levy a tax upon the enterprise in which he invests his money together with a voice in the control of it. Thus the grip of profit-seeking capital upon industry will be loosened.[1]

We must go further. The investor gets his interest; the workman gets his wages. There is no reason why the former should also get a share in the control and the latter should not. Labour has historically been very reluctant to accept a share in the control of industry or the direction of its policy. It is doubtful whether Labour at present would generally accept its proportion of places on the Boards of Directors or make a very good use of those places if it did.[2] There is need on any showing for a new enterprise of planning in Industry and this must obviously be undertaken by the State. It may be that Labour will best exercise its control, at any rate at first, through

[1] See Note 2 on p. 58.
[2] See Note 3 on p. 60.

the organ of Government responsible for this.

Meanwhile great transformations are going on before our eyes. There is growing up a great section of society—Industrial Management—which has many of the characteristics of a profession or a civil service.[1] In a planned economy, Management would inevitably be responsible to the State as much as to Directors representing shareholders, and the State would have to nominate members of the Boards of Directors. Thus alike in the general plan and in the particular administration the consumer through the State would have his effective voice.

One more modification of the present system may be mentioned as required by social justice: wherever limitation of liability is granted it should be accompanied by limitation of profits. The Articles of Association should provide for the allocation of surplus profits to such purposes as these: an equalization fund for the maintenance of wages in bad times, even though hours of work be reduced; a similar fund for the maintenance of interest to shareholders at a specified minimum; a sinking fund for the repayment of invested capital; a fund for the extension of fixed capital, and so forth. Thus investor and workman gain greater security and the urge to secure maximum profits is mitigated.[2]

If we are to move in this direction some action is

[1] See Note 4 on p 61.
[2] See Note 5 on p. 62.

required now. The first is an act of resolve that the controls over private enterprise, established for war-time purposes, shall be retained when peace returns. They will, of course, call for modification; but they must not be abolished. Secondly, they must be used at once to ensure deferred spending, so that inflation may be avoided and the wealthier classes may not appropriate an unfair share of the now limited amount of available goods. Justice seems to require that this should be accompanied by a scheme of Family Allowances—to begin, perhaps, with the third child born in one family.

There is one further necessary change. No scheme of publicly organized production can be satisfactory apart from national control of credit. We all have reason to be grateful for the stability of our Banking system and for the ability and integrity with which it is administered. Yet it cannot be justified in modern conditions that the Banks, even the Bank of England, should, in order to meet national needs, create credit which earns interest for themselves. "The State must resume the right to control the issue and cancellation of every kind of money." Till that is done, a body within the community will control what is vital to the welfare of the community; and that is a false principle.[1]

I offer these proposals not as dogmas but as matter for discussion and as indications of a spirit rather

---

[1] See Note 6 on p. 63.

than as a definite policy. It may be that there are other and better ways of attaining our object. But our object is clear: it is to reverse that reversal of the natural order, which is characteristic of our phase of civilization; the natural order is that consumption should control production and production should utilize finance. And this must be done in the way that will most secure both freedom and order, both initiative and security, and may promote the only real progress, which is the development of personality in fellowship.

NOTE 1

If it is thought desirable to exempt agricultural land from death duties, recent legislation makes the choice of land for this purpose quite easy; it should be that land which is scheduled for de-rating. And, of course, if any of it is sold, the purchase money must at once become subject to death duties.

Some socialists are horrified by this proposed exemption. Their policy of land-nationalization is, of course, quite consistent. Personally I am convinced that it would work out very badly. As a nation we are not good at detailed organization, though when roused by a great need we can give a splendid exhibition of efficiency. But the bane of our democracy is the red-tape in the clerical departments of national and municipal offices. To let this loose upon rural England would lead to calamity.

The present system combines all the disadvantages.

We leave the private landlord in possession and make it impossible for him properly to discharge the social responsibilities of his station.

NOTE 2

It is interesting and very instructive to see how the application of the same principle to different circumstances may find expression in diametrically opposite enactments. Thus the medieval theologian could tolerate marginal profits but absolutely condemned debentures; he regarded those profits as a balance to the risk, usually considerable in those days, of possible total loss. Limited liability had not been invented! His objection to what we call debentures was that the money lent was earning interest (or, as he said, " breeding ") while the principal was safe and undiminished. Professor Tawney, on the same ethical grounds as were taken by the medieval theologians, is ready to tolerate debentures (where the interest is payment for the service rendered in allowing the use of the capital and the shareholder does not acquire a permanent hold on the concern) but condemns marginal profits in these days of relative security as encouraging exploitation, and most of all condemns the rents received by urban ground-landlords as payment given where no service is rendered. (See *The Acquisitive Society,* Chapter V.)

In the same way it will be noticed that in one particular I suggest an inversion of the Law of Jubilee; but this is done to preserve its essence. The Levitical Law allowed the sale in perpetuity, and therefore also the purchase in perpetuity, of an urban house (Leviticus xxv. 29-30), but forbade this in the case of agricultural land and the houses upon it (30, 31). The reason for this prohibition was a desire to retain the family property and prevent the extrusion of the less prosperous and formation of large estates at their expense—a process condemned also by Isaiah (v. 8). A vivid account of the Mosaic Legislation concerning Economics can be found in *My Neighbour's Landmark* by Verinder, lately republished by the Henry George Foundation.

In the modern world a mass of small owners could not be either prosperous or secure. I suggest a safeguarding of tradition and of family connexion with agricultural land by exempting it from death duties, and a gradual elimination of urban ground-landlords by drastic death duties—with permission to pay these by the direct cession of part of the estate to the national or municipal authority. I should forbid the sale of urban land except to the public authority. Thus, for example, the London County Council would in course of time become the ground-landlord of London, and could then use the ground rents for public services, either extending these accordingly or reducing rates by the amount of the ground rents. Functionless property is unjustified and should be eliminated.

But there should be no mere confiscation. The new order must not be introduced with callous indifference to reasonable expectations encouraged by the old order. The fair way of effecting the transition is not easy to find.

As existing expectations when reasonable should be treated with respect and sympathy, though not always completely satisfied, so unreasonable expectations should be thwarted. One of these is the expectation of turning to private profit the additional value which land may acquire through the enterprise of others or through communal activity. The best suggestion known to me here is that a general valuation of all land should be made as soon as possible, and no sale at a higher price than this, nor rent at more than a fair percentage of this, be permissible, unless it can be shown that an increase in value has been caused by the action of the landlord.

Note 3

The claim to an effective share in the control of industry is an avowed object—on paper—of many Trade Unions. They have been curiously unwilling to shoulder the responsibility when any opportunity has been given. The fact is that they were constituted to deal with the chief problems of the nineteenth century and are structurally and psychologically ill-adapted for the chief opportunities of to-day. They are concerned to maintain standards of hours, wages and conditions for those who are in work. This was once the chief need of the working-class; it is still a real need but no longer the chief. The chief need now is to gain security of employment. The Trade Unions are ready to pass resolutions about the " right to work ", but accept next to no responsibility for their members who fall out of employment. Their impotence in face of the grave unemployment of 1931-1933 was evidence that they are not, as now constituted, adequate to the need. It is a natural consequence of this that they produce few leaders able to take a strong personal initiative. For the first thing a strong Labour leader must do is to remodel the Union of which he is an official. He will find that it is exactly as difficult to overcome the vested interests of Labour organizations and those who gain a living by working them as it is to overcome the capitalist vested interests which Labour rightly denounces. The source of the trouble is not wealth; it is sin—which is the perquisite of no class, and (incidentally) besets us who are ecclesiastical officials as much as others.

NOTE 4

It is difficult to exaggerate the importance of the position in Modern Industry of the Manager. He is as a rule the key man, whether he is a Director or not. Certainly the great Managing Directors tend to rule the Boards of which they are at once members and servants. The present system makes them technically the employés of the Directors representing the Shareholders. When industrial strife threatens they meet, in this capacity, the Trade Union Secretaries as representing Labour. But all their interest is in the actual process of production, not in its incidental financial results. Wise reform will aim at an arrangement which brings them as close as possible to the active factors in production. If there is to be tension at all, let it be between the financial interests of Shareholders and the productive interests of Management and Labour in co-operation. We must secure that all those actively engaged in production feel themselves, and feel one another, to be partners in a common enterprise.

If this were carried out universally it would inaugurate a system of National Guilds or Guild Socialism. The principle of that system has much to commend it. But it is certainly a mistake to begin with the picture of a supposedly ideal system and try to establish it. The way of Christian progress is to ask where an existing system is breaking down and readjust it in the light of Christian principles.

NOTE 5

This scheme for limiting profits where liability is limited was keenly advocated by the early Christian Socialists when Joint Stock Companies were beginning to be formed. It would have saved the world much evil if their warnings had been heeded.

I have been asked if I have considered how these changes would affect charitable societies and the like which hold stock as the endowment for their work. Of course I have! How could an Ecclesiastical Commissioner do otherwise? I think they must be prepared for some considerable financial loss. But as with ownership of site-values, there should be no mere confiscation. Either the shares now held should be converted into debentures and made repayable at a certain date, when the money could be re-invested, or else a series of operations similar to the recent Tithe Act should be carried through, whereby the State would redeem the existing shares. It need not be done all at once!

NOTE 6

I have touched very briefly on the immense subject of Money and Credit. I am sure it is vital, but rather than go into further detail myself I will refer the reader to Sir Reginald Rowe's admirable statement *The Root of All Evil*, published by the Economic Reform Club, which may be ordered from any branch of Messrs. W. H. Smith and Son.

To these Notes on particular passages in the preceding talk I will add one which is more general. I have received letters urging that the first duty of an ecclesiastic is to bring reasonable order into the financial system of the Church. Those who so write seldom show any awareness how much in history and in law can be quoted against them. But I cordially agree with them; and I take this opportunity of commending to any who are concerned about this matter the admirable pamphlet *Men, Money and the Ministry*.

VI

A Christian Civilization

If what I have said in the previous talks of this series is at all true, our hope for a new world must be based on faith in God, and pursued in accordance with His character and law. In other words, it must be a hope for a truly Christian civilization. It has often been said that we are fighting for a Christian civilization; my whole contention is that it is our duty to prove that to be a true claim. For this purpose, it is not enough only to preserve our inheritance. The civilization which we knew in our country before the war was deeply influenced by Christian principles; and its Christian quality is precisely that which would be lost by a Nazi triumph and the reshaping of our life in subordination to the policy of a Nazi conqueror. But it fell short at too many points to be called, without qualification, a Christian civilization. For at least half a century its predominant culture has been what is called Humanism, which consists, roughly speaking, in the acceptance of many Christian standards of life with a rejection or neglect of the only sources of power to attain to them. The result was a decline from those standards in all respects in which conformity to them involved serious self-discipline. Indeed, at one point, we were sinking into real decadence; for it is a signal mark of decadence when people are more troubled by pain than by sin, by suffering than by moral evil. The war has shown that this had not gone very deep. We can all to-day choose suffering rather than disloyalty, without a shadow of hesitation. But, before the war, the perplexity, of which people were conscious in relation to God's government of the world, was caused far more by the prevalence of suffering than by the prevalence of selfishness; and that is a very bad sign. In our estimate of the relative importance of duty and pleasure, of wickedness and pain, we are far more Christian now than we were a year ago.

We are not fighting so much to preserve a Christian civilization, as for the opportunity to make one. What then do we mean by a Christian civilization? The words could be used to describe a perfect system worked by perfect citizens. Obviously we do not mean that, for it is unattainable. We mean a civilization in which the Christian standards of value are accepted as those by which both persons and policies are to be judged, and in which there is a steady effort to guide policy by Christian principles. It is not required, in order that our civilization may be called Christian, that we should never fail to live and to order life by those principles; it is required that we should steadily try, and seek to recover ground recognized as lost when we consciously or unconsciously depart from them.

If we are to advance in this direction, three conditions must be met.

First, education must be effectively Christian. It is a sad fact—largely due to the divisions among Christians—that though the Foreign Secretary declares that we are fighting for Christian civilization, yet when the Board of Education launches a Youth Movement it cannot say that its aim is to train Christian citizens. It is indispensable that Christians should reach sufficient agreement among themselves for the State to act on their united witness; and I believe we are very near to that now.

Secondly, Christians must actively co-operate with all who share their convictions with regard to policy and action, even though these do not share the faith on which, for Christians, these are grounded.

Thirdly, there must be a body of people inspired by genuine Christian faith and eager to think out and act upon its implications for personal and public life. This, of course, involves much study and thought. Christian industrialists and business men should get together, along with some economists and one or two theologians, to work out what is really involved for their own part of the nation's life in the convictions which must lie at the root of any enterprise on behalf of a Christian civilization; for all who care about this, the *Christian News-Letter*[1] will be found invaluable.

Some of these Christian convictions can be set out as follows:

(1) There is an order of the world and of life in which men and women and their various activities have their place. It is a natural order, in the sense that it gives a proper place to each person or function according to the best service which can be given to the life of the whole. This is Plato's principle of Justice; for the Christian it is a divinely appointed order, because God is Creator of the world; but it can

[1] Edited by J. H. Oldham. Obtainable from Arlosh Hall, Mansfield Road, Oxford.

be in very large measure ascertained without any conscious reference to God, as will be seen as we pass on.

(2) Man is a part of the system of nature, whatever else he may be beside. He must study the ways of nature and follow them, for he is utterly dependent on the natural world. Consequently, he must not think of natural resources as there for him to exploit to his own immediate advantage, but must rather co-operate with the natural process and so, in the long run, gain a far greater advantage. This is of primary importance in relation to man's treatment of the soil. Nature is man's partner rather than his servant; he is dependent on it for the means of life. For the Christian this is recognized as a pact of creatureship. The treatment of the earth by man the exploiter is not only imprudent but sacrilegious. We are not likely to correct our hideous mistakes in this realm unless we can recover the mystical sense of our one-ness with nature. I labour this precisely because many people think it fantastic; I think it is fundamental to sanity.

(3) Within human society we must aim at establishing that relation of the various functions or activities to one another which corresponds to their contribution to the general well-being. Thus a land-owner must not be allowed to develop his land for his own profit in a way which destroys its capacity to produce wealth or otherwise minister to the general good for generations to come. In this connexion, let us remember that natural beauty is a spiritual treasure;

to convert it into ugliness for personal economic gain is wicked; to intrude upon it in order to bring employment and comfort to a multitude may be justifiable, but only if no other way is possible. Again, money exists to facilitate the exchange of goods; it must not be so controlled as to increase the gains of those who hold it at the cost of diminishing the exchange of goods.

If men were perfect, we should not have to think out how we may prevent these departures from the natural order; they would, of themselves, almost automatically establish a social order corresponding to the natural order. But because men tend to put their own advantage before the general good, and, even when they put the general good first, tend to interpret this in the light of their own interest and that of their own friends, there is need of action by the public authority to establish and maintain both individual conduct and a social order that corresponds as closely as may be to that natural order. In this, as in all its activity, the method of the State is so to order life with sanctions and penalties, that the lower motives in men's souls are enlisted in support of that conduct which the higher motives prompt. If I am honest, I shall pay my debts by free choice; but if I am dishonest, I shall still pay my debts for fear of the inconveniences that follow from refusal to do so. There is then nothing morally good about my action; but the right act is done.

We shall not, in fact, advance towards a really Christian civilization unless there is a large body of convinced Christians urging the whole community that way. How can we present to ourselves the constant inspiration that they will need? For they will need inspiration—the guidance and power of the Holy Spirit. I am sure that what is wanted is a close and evident connexion between secular life and worship. I will express what seems to me to be required, by using as a figure that form of religious service which our Lord appointed for His disciples, and which perfectly represents the central truths which must be constantly before us; and this figure must be considered in two ways. We usually think of the Holy Communion in association only with God's act in Redemption; we must also think of it in connexion with His act in Creation. Then the power that guides and sustains us will be indeed the Holy Spirit proceeding from the Father and the Son.

In that service we take bread and wine. What are these? They are the perfect symbol of the economic life of man. Before there can be bread the land must be ploughed, the seed scattered, the harvest gathered, the corn threshed, the flour baked; and before all that, there must be the gift of God in the life of the seed, the nurturing quality of the soil, sunshine and rain. Bread is an instance of God's gifts made available by human labour for the satisfaction of men's needs. The same is true of wine. In the production of these things, man co-operates with God. The farmer who cares for his land and neglects his prayers is, as a farmer, co-operating with God; and the farmer who says his prayers but neglects his land is failing, as a farmer, to co-operate with God. It is a great mistake to suppose that God is only, or even chiefly, concerned with religion. But of course the truly Christian farmer cares for land and prayers alike.

In the Holy Communion service we take the bread and wine—man's industrial and commercial life in symbol—and offer it to God; because we have offered it to Him, He gives it back to us as the means of nurturing us, not in our animal nature alone, but as agents of His purpose, limbs of a body responsive to His will; and as we receive it back from Him, we share it with one another in true fellowship. If we think of the service in this way, it is a perfect picture of what secular society ought to be; and a Christian civilization is one where the citizens seek to make their ordered life something of which that service is the symbol.

But this is not enough. The sin of man's nature, his self-centredness, is so deeply rooted in him that it is quite impossible for him, by his own act of will, to direct his life by such principles as we have described. What he chiefly needs is not guidance but redemption. Something must be done for him and in him that he can never do himself. Therefore, if there is to be a Christian civilization, we need not only citizens who have the right picture of society, but also enough citizens who have found the redeeming power that is in Christ. These will use the Holy Communion in the way we have described, but with another thought as well. They take the bread and wine as Christ took them in the night of His betrayal. He took the bread, called it His body and broke it; He took the wine, called it His blood and gave it. We do what He did that we may be united to Him in His self-giving, and may receive through His Broken Body the power to give ourselves unto death, and through His Blood— His life sacrificially offered—may receive the life which is not destroyed by death but rather released by it that it may be united to God for ever.

If there is to be a Christian civilization, there must be a body of Christians dedicated to God and His Kingdom in a manner of which the Holy Communion, so regarded, is the picture, and for which it offers the spiritual strength.

I end these talks with a call to Christian people to pledge themselves in this way. Let us become conscious of ourselves as a fellowship pledged to God and to one another to stand and contend for international and social justice; to set little store by our possessions and much by our responsibilities; to seek, in worship, at once the understanding of our task and the quality by which we may perform it; to make use of the service appointed by our Lord as the symbol of our social life and the means of our personal dedication; and daily to commit ourselves, our country and all mankind to God in the prayer our Lord has taught us. Let all of us spend five minutes every day in this act of recollection and committal, if possible in a church where concentration will be easier, but if not there then elsewhere; and let us pray as He taught us, trying each day to think out more fully the meaning of what we say. The prayer will be to our Father—my Father who loves me, but the Father also of all other men. Let us be sure that the double thought expressed in those two words is always in our minds. Then every week on Sunday let us think especially of the words, "Hallowed be Thy name", picturing what the world would be like if that came true throughout all nations; on Monday—"Thy Kingdom come"; on Tuesday— "Thy will be done". On Wednesday we will pray especially for daily bread—not mine or yours, but *our* daily bread, the need of all God's children; on Thursday for forgiveness—as we forgive; on Friday for freedom from unnecessary temptation and deliverance from the evil which has a hold on us; and on Saturday we will remember for whose glory we ask all this and in whose power we can accomplish it.

If there is a great fellowship of people really praying like this, they will transform our country, for real prayer means real purpose and wins the strength to accomplish it. Some people may like to symbolize this fellowship in prayer and dedication by wearing some token that each can make for himself, such as a little cross of wood or other material. But that is not essential. This fellowship of prayer exists already. Let us pledge ourselves to it, and to a life in conformity with it.

Our hope for a new world is in Him who declares from the throne of Heaven, "Behold, I make all things new."

II

THE ARMOUR OF GOD

Take up the whole armour of God, that ye may be able to withstand in the evil day, and, having done all, to stand.—Ephesians vi. 13.

In these days the whole future history of Europe is at stake. Upon the issue of the conflict now joined the quality of civilization in the coming period depends. Our hearts and minds are with the brave men from our country, from France and from Belgium and the gallant remnant from Holland, now resisting the onslaught of an embattled tyranny, whose success would make impossible the achievement of our best hopes for our country and the world, and would destroy the best that our fathers have bequeathed to us.

At such a moment, called by our King, we turn to God. We commend our cause to God; we dedicate ourselves to Him.

Our cause is the cause of freedom and mutual trust. The immediate occasion of our entry into the war was an attack made upon Poland in direct breach of a pledge deliberately offered by those who afterwards broke it. This was only the last of a whole series of broken pledges. If this policy of promise and betrayal is allowed to succeed, there is an end of good fellowship among the peoples of different nations for many a year to come.

With this method of the broken promise goes contempt for the rights of the weak and the small. In such a world there can be no justice and no freedom. The supreme excellences of our inherited civilization must then disappear, and it might be that centuries would pass before they could be recovered. We have not at all times served justice, freedom and truth as we should; we too are sinners; but we have so far believed in these things and honoured them that an appeal to them is never without effect in our country, and when the issue has been clear we have ranged ourselves on their side. If we are to strive worthily for these great principles, we must dedicate ourselves to them more deeply than in the past and serve them in the coming days more consistently. But the first necessity is to save them from extinction; and the success of our enemies would mean their extinction at least for many generations.

For the German Government, which has shown its contempt for justice, truth and freedom in its dealing with other nations, has shown the same contempt in its internal administration. Freedom is abolished in practice and repudiated in theory; truth is suppressed and replaced by propaganda; justice is explicitly declared to be such treatment of each individual as may best serve the interest of the State; and that is a sheer denial of all that we mean by justice. But it follows at once from that exaltation of the State as an object of absolute and final loyalty which is essential to National Socialism. Against this idolatry we must proclaim that only to God is absolute loyalty due; and God is the Father of all men, so that His children have their value and worth independently of any earthly allegiance, and all alike are entitled to fair dealing. What we have learnt to understand by justice is rooted and grounded in the sovereignty of God.

We are fighting then to keep open the possibility of a civilization governed by Christian principles; we are fighting for the opportunity to make the ordering of human life increasingly Christian. Certainly it is right that those who are engaged in such a cause should commend that cause to God. For it is His cause; we can serve it worthily, only if we serve it in loyalty to Him. It is God's cause; and He will not let it fail. By what course He will bring it to victory we cannot know. It may be, as our hearts yearn that it may be, by speedy success; it may be through long struggle and with hope long deferred. It cannot be claimed that, because our cause is God's cause, it will triumph quickly or without loss. Christ won His Kingdom by the Cross, and on the first Good Friday evening it looked as if His cause was dead. Yet be-

77

cause of the way in which He bore it, the Cross, which
for the moment stood for the victory of evil, stands
evermore for the victory of good. We must strive
with all our energy and exhaust our strength as we resist by physical force the evil force which seeks to
overthrow civilization and carry us back to barbarism;
yet even more essential to the cause we serve than all
material resources is the spirit in which we use them.
Vitally important as it is that by any sacrifice which
may be needed the men and munitions be forthcoming, it is still more important than this earthly
armament that we put on the whole armour of
God.

It is for this that we are called to prayer as a nation.
But let us be quite clear that when we turn to prayer,
it cannot be as Britons who happen to be Christians;
it must be as Christians who happen to be British.
Otherwise we fall into the error of our enemies, whose
distinctive sin it is that they put nationality first. It
is quite true that the British Empire is at stake; if we
are defeated it is doomed. And that Empire, in spite
of some dark pages in its history and many imperfec-
tions in its present life, is yet the bearer of a tradition
so noble and so precious to mankind that duty would
call us to fight for its preservation, even if nothing
further were at stake. Yet in our prayers we must
think first, not of the British Empire, but of the
world-wide family of God. It is for the hope and
opportunity to work for the peace and goodwill of

that great family that we strive; it is for the realization of that hope that we pray.

We pray to Our Father, the Father of all mankind, that He will enable us to preserve for all His family the justice, freedom and love of truth which are threatened now. We pray that His Name may be hallowed in all the world—in Russia where men deny it altogether, in Germany where they take it in vain, and in our own country, where our reverence has been but half-hearted. We pray that His Kingdom may come, that men may everywhere obey His laws so that He is manifestly King of the world that He has made —in Germany where the sovereignty of the God of all the earth has been identified with the supremacy of the German State, in our own country where regard for self-interest and love of ease have largely taken the place of obedience to God. We pray that His will may be done, His purpose of righteous love fulfilled, unspoilt by the selfishness and hatreds of men—in Germany where hatred of some races has been taught as a patriotic duty, in our own country where love has so far failed that we still acquiesce in even large-scale unemployment as a normal feature of our national life.

Our prayer is for God's will to be done throughout the world and that He will use us for the doing of it. If our prayer is real it must express a true dedication. We cannot dedicate ourselves to the doing of so much of God's will as suits our own convenience. In this day of judgment when men's neglect of God and His laws has led to calamity beyond words to express and to anxiety that wrings the heart, we need dedication complete and absolute. It must include in its object the purposes of God beyond this war; but in these present days it must be dedication to the task of fighting to hold open the opportunity of justice, freedom and truth.

Even now the war has not profoundly affected the daily lives of multitudes. We need a more searching self-discipline than we have as yet accepted, by which to keep constantly effective that firmness of resolution which has been present from the outset. We are being tested; we need the utmost strength that we can gain; and the source of surest strength, steadfastness and perseverance is faith in God and dedication to the doing of His will. Let each of us say in his heart, in the words suggested by the Dean of St. Paul's: "It all depends on me; and I depend on God."

Sorrow is coming to our homes as it did not come in the first days of the war. Where is real comfort for such sorrow to be found except in fellowship with Christ, who endured bitter anguish in unfailing love, and thereby brought into the world its only hope of deliverance from bitterness and strife and of entry into the reign of love and peace on which our hope is set?

Confident, therefore, because we have offered our cause and ourselves to God, strengthened to endure whatever of grief or pain our service of the just cause may bring, we go forward to throw back the enemies of freedom and truth, and to do our part in establishing justice, freedom and truth throughout the world.

"Is there any hope," some ask, "that those who have engaged in war with all its horrors can really serve that cause? Will they not become vindictive, so that when they have held the door open for advance in the ways of justice and freedom, they will be unable to pass through it, and will fail the cause they have fought to save?" The danger is real. It is hard to fight with all one's might and still avoid all hatred. But it is possible on one condition; it is the condition which we are to-day called to fulfil—the realization of our dependence upon God and the committing of our cause and ourselves to Him. This is not a task for one day only; our national day of prayer can only have its full effect if it is a focusing point for prayer which is continuous and constant.

We are not worthy to be God's instruments; there is much in us for which we must ask forgiveness. He offers that forgiveness in the continuance of His trust, as He trusts us still to serve Him, though He knows our unworthiness better than we do. Yet He makes one demand; He forgives us as we forgive. We are called to the hardest of all tasks: to fight without hatred, to resist without bitterness, and in the end, if God grant it so, to triumph without vindictiveness.

We cannot do this by ourselves; we can only do it

in the strength of God. So to-day we lay our cause, our allies, our country and ourselves in the hands of God, praying that He will use us in the battle for justice, freedom and truth, keeping us brave, nerving us for sacrifice, and crowning our effort with the triumph of that for which we fight, and the establishment of a brotherhood of nations where justice, truth and freedom shall be secure.

III

OUR HOPE FOR THE FUTURE

EVERYONE recognizes that the present period is one of the turning-points of human history. This war is not a dog-fight between national imperialisms; it is a struggle between two incompatible ways of life. Of course it is true that purely national interests are involved; it may even be true that Great Britain finally took its stand only when its own interests were obviously menaced. At first these considerations loomed so large that they obscured from the minds of many people the questions which are really at stake. This was particularly true of some idealists on both sides of the Atlantic. We were told that we could not be really serving any sound principle, because we were so evidently guided by self-interest.

About this I should like to say two things, because they have a great bearing on my main argument. First, there has been a very strong body of opinion in England which was ready to support a more disinterested policy in the whole of the last twenty years, and many have rallied to this since the war broke out. But secondly, the whole way of looking at the matter which prompts this detachment is morally unsound; if I see a house burning and know there is a child in it, I must not delay any action to save that child until I am sure that I have no desire for admiration or other reward contaminating my altruistic motives. The important matter is that the child should be saved. So now—the important matter is that freedom should be saved. Whatever may be said about rival imperialisms, and I will say some of this in a moment, no one acquainted with life in Great Britain and in Germany during the last seven years, or with the change in the life of Czecho-Slovakia, Poland, Denmark, Norway, Holland, Belgium and France, since they came under Nazi rule, can possibly doubt that this rule is a tyranny which has extended its sway by conquest and threatens to extend it further. Of course the war is not a conflict between pure light and unmitigated darkness; but it is a conflict between freedom and tyranny; and the whole world is involved in it. If Europe as a whole passes under Nazi rule, freedom will not survive elsewhere without a fearful struggle. What is now in the balance is the future of European and American civilization for the next long epoch of its history. If that is the fact, all questions concerning the motives of the British Government a year ago are an academic irrelevance, and convict those who raise them of superficiality and levity of mind. They have nothing whatever to do with the crisis confronting mankind.

OUR HOPE FOR THE FUTURE

There is much in British history and in contemporary British life which is open to criticism from a standpoint of high idealism. We ought to be grateful to those who remind us of these things and so keep our consciences alert. But these defects, even when they are defects in liberty itself, do not alter the fact that broadly speaking the British flag has stood for steadily increasing liberty, and an appeal to the principle of liberty never goes unheeded in Great Britain, even when the action called for is delayed.

Misunderstanding is sometimes caused by a casual and inaccurate use of language. I have known some Englishmen misled by the common habit of describing some parts of the earth as " belonging to " Great Britain. No part of the earth "belongs to " Great Britain in the sense in which a man's house and garden belong to him. So far as the British Government undertakes the control and direction of (for example) some parts of Equatorial Africa, it always regards it as a solemn obligation to train the indigenous peoples towards self-government as members of the family of civilized nations. Sometimes things are done under pressure of private interest which cut across this steady purpose; the British Empire shares with other human institutions an inability to be at all times true to its own best principles. But the principles are accepted; the steady purpose is there; and progress in liberty and training for the use of it is constant even though somewhat patchy.

The great Empire of India illustrates the same principle. I personally wish that we moved faster than we do, but the series of legislative acts affecting India since the responsibility of the East India Company was transferred to the British Crown has tended steadily in one direction—the direction of advance towards self-government. I want to go faster, as I have said; but the direction in which we have moved is right from the standpoint of all who love freedom. I wish that the Act of 1935, by which the present constitution of India was established, had gone much further than it did; but even as it was, it took its place among a very few legislative acts whereby so large a concession of power has at any time been made by any ruling nation.

In the case of the Dominions the principle of self-government receives complete expression. In no sense whatever does Canada belong to Great Britain. Equally with Great Britain it gives allegiance to the British Throne; equally with Great Britain it belongs to the British Empire. Great Britain does not possess the Dominions; it is the senior member in an equal partnership. The present neutrality of Eire and the hesitation of South Africa at the outset whether or not to declare war on Germany remind us that the great part now taken in the war by the Dominions is taken by their own free choice.

This Commonwealth of Nations, embodying the principle of freedom in a fellowship which girdles the earth, is engaged in deadly conflict with a German Reich which is at this moment subject to a government and a doctrine for which the whole principle of liberty is abhorrent. I need not specify the features of the Nazi system which stamp it as the foe of freedom—the Gestapo, the Concentration Camps, the declared policy concerning coloured peoples. Our hostility to the Nazi regime is directed not only against its acts, but against its principles. We often fail to practise what we preach; but we can be recalled to our avowed principles. They do preach what they practise, and all appeal to them in the name of principles sacred to us is futile.

In face of this conflict a Christian cannot doubt or hesitate. Christianity, as is clear from the Gospels, stakes everything on human freedom. Christians have often failed to recognize this; but the Gospel-message is clear. Man cannot save himself; there is something that must be done for him. But neither can man be saved despite himself, and he can reject the salvation offered to him. The Gospels show Christ everywhere paying to the free personality of men and women a respect and trust which nothing—not even the intended treachery of Judas—could shake. Freedom is a necessary element in the foundation of a Christian civilization because it is the first presupposition of Christianity itself.

We are not fighting for Christianity; that must always be both wrong and futile. But we are fighting to maintain an order of society which gives free course to the Christian Gospel and offers a hope of advance towards a truly Christian civilization. Of course the ideal properly so described can never be fully realized on earth; but it is not impossible to reach a state of affairs where Christian principles are accepted by the greater part of the population, and public opinion takes them as the standard of judgment upon policy. We have not reached that point yet. But it is clear that a Nazi victory would postpone for so long as it was effective any advance towards the fulfilment of such a hope.

At this point the question may be raised whether a victory of Great Britain and her Allies would really open the way. Why should not this war be followed by another Versailles Treaty, a repetition of the years 1920-39, and another outbreak of European war expanding into world war? My answer would be in three stages. First, the Nazi threat is not only to such liberty and justice as we hope to see, but also to that which we have already established. It is worth while to fight in order to keep the Gestapo out of Great Britain and to turn it out of France, Holland and the rest. Secondly, it is true that victory in war cannot by itself inaugurate the better time; it can only make the new dawn possible; but this it can and will do. Thirdly, we have learnt much from the experience of the last twenty years, alike from failure and from success. The League of Nations has not been a total failure; its social services, especially on the medical side, have been invaluable; and where it failed we see the source of the failure and can largely avoid a repetition. Particularly we see the impossibility of regulating the political relations of countries while ignoring their economic relations.

If we can start the work of reconstruction on the basis of two principles, respect for personal liberty and co-operation in establishing for the masses of the people in all countries a secure share in the wealth now so abundantly available, we shall inaugurate a new era of fellowship and international partnership which may well gain for mankind a future of security, peace and goodwill.

Victory makes that possible; without victory there can be no such hope. Let us then make sure of victory that we may also devote ourselves to the fulfilment of that hope.

IV

PRINCIPLES OF RECONSTRUCTION

THE only excuse which I can have for taking part in a discussion of " Europe after the War " is the hope of illustrating one direction in which Christian principles seem to point us. I am far from claiming that the suggestions which I offer are the only available application of Christian principles; and I fully recognize that the right time for an action is as important as the quality of the action itself, so that even those who share my hopes may regard my practical suggestions as impracticable or premature. But I hold that Christians are responsible for endeavouring to apply the principles of their faith to the actual problems of life, regarding them not as a source of direct instructions, but as an indication of the goal to be aimed at and as a standard of judgment to which policy must be referred.

The relevant principles, I think, are these:

(1) Every man is a child of God and as such has a status and dignity independent of his membership in any earthly state.

(2) Consequently, personality is sacred, and freedom in whatever is most personal (worship, thought, expression) is to be safeguarded as among the primary ends for which the State exists.

(3) As children of God, men are members of one family, and life should be ordered as far as possible with a view to the promotion of brotherly fellowship among all men, while each is called upon to use his freedom in the spirit of "membership" on pain of forfeiting his moral right to it.

(4) But men are not dutiful children of God. They are from birth self-centred, and remain so in lesser or greater degrees. They can be delivered from this evil state only by the active love (grace) of God calling out surrender and trust (faith). So far as this has not happened or has incompletely happened—(*i.e.* universally)—they need to be restrained in their self-assertiveness and induced by appeals to their self-interest to respect justice in their mutual dealings.

(5) Nations exist by God's providential guidance of history and have their part to play in His purpose; but man's self-centredness infects his national loyalty, which in its own nature is wholesome, so that the nation is made an object of that absolute allegiance which is due to God alone. Thus, if there is to be any approach to a brotherly fellowship of nations before all men are converted to a life of perfect love, it must be by the same method of so organizing their relation-

ship to one another that national self-interest will itself urge justice in action.

Approaching the matter in this way, I attach the greatest importance to the growing strength of the conviction and feeling among all Christians that they are united in and through Christ in a perfect fellowship. Without this I do not expect to see any living and enduring sense of fellowship between the nations. As yet this "ecumenical sense" is feeble; but it is growing fast. It is a main ground of hope for the Rebirth of Christendom in the future. If it continues to grow it will supply in every nation where the Church is planted a nucleus of the spirit of true fellowship which will be of priceless value in binding the nations together.

The two first principles stated above give strong support to some form of democracy as the constitution best suited for developing and expressing the quality of "personality" in its citizens. It would be excessive to say that they "demand" this, for the primary function of a political constitution is to ensure that good order without which free personal life is almost impossible. Insecurity due to outbreaks of mob-violence is if anything more incompatible with effective freedom of personal living than tyrannous rule by a Government of which the principles, and consequently its occasions of tyrannous action, are at least known. Not all peoples have been able to maintain order through democratic institutions; and unless they can, it is futile to say that a theological principle " demands " democracy.

But it can and must be said that where people are ready to work democratic institutions, they more fully conform to the principle of the sanctity of personality than any other type. The main point to be secured is that the people should have the opportunity to change the Government without breaking up the Constitution, so that effective " opposition " to the Government of the day is perfectly compatible with loyalty to nation and to State. Only so can a free play of personal judgment be encouraged and exercised.

Consequently it may be laid down that any new order which is established must be " safe for democracy ". No nation will be coerced into democracy; but it must be open to every nation to adopt it. (It seems likely that a German victory would result in the exact opposite of this.)

The third principle—the unity of all men in the " family " of God—points to an organization of life which draws together in relations of mutual support the largest practicable number of persons. But emphasis must be laid on the word " practicable ". It cannot be inferred from this principle without more ado that a large State is always preferable to a small State or that if any system of federation is adopted, the more States to be federated the better. The reality of mutual interdependence may be more complete in a small society, and the forcing together of those who have no desire to co-operate is a sure road to calamity. But the principle will at once put us on our guard against the notion of a State founded on and bounded by racial homogeneity; for such a State will be subject in a quite special degree to the temptations of self-centred acquisitiveness and aggression. On the whole the balance of advantage seems to lie with a union or federation of States, each small enough to give to the citizens a sense of individual responsibility for its welfare, while the whole group is large enough to combine many peoples of rather diverse traditions and interests, so that these may balance and check one another.

For the fourth and fifth principles remind us that no system, however cunningly devised, will work smoothly to the general satisfaction unless it contains within itself elements which balance and hold back the unexorcized egotism of individuals and, still more, of all collective groups of men. The civilized State secures a substantial measure of justice in the lives of its citizens by attaching penalties to unjust action, so that self-interest itself prompts avoidance of injustice and pursuit of justice. Even those of us who are usually honest on principle and by preference, are occasionally saved from lapses into dishonesty by the penalties attached to it when detected. But the egotism of a nation is infinitely greater than that of an individual; for in any individual there are instincts and impulses tending to generosity and social conduct. But the nation appeals first to those very impulses as it demands of its citizens self-sacrifice in its service, and then to the impulses of self-assertion as it urges them to gird themselves to battle with its and their enemies. It appeals to love and to hatred, both at once, with the result that the nation itself, in its contrast with and opposition to other nations, can become demoniac in its egotism.

The cure for this, short of the leavening influence of an effective universal Church, seems to lie in a profitable union and organized co-operation of peoples sufficiently close in tradition and interest for this to be voluntarily accepted, yet sufficiently disparate to introduce some efficient checks and balances. How far contiguous national groups provide opportunity for this is a matter for the political specialist. But I suggest that some groups stand out as offering these characteristics in greater or less degree: (a) the Danubian group; (b) Germany, if freed from the Prussian domination over the other constituent parts of the Reich; (c) the Czechs, Slovaks and Poles; (d) the Scandinavian countries; (e) Great Britain and France, with, perhaps, Belgium, Luxembourg and Holland.

It is not suggested that all these groups can be at once established after the war. But it seems most unlikely that a general federation of Europe can be effected then either, and to propose as a means to this (which would best accord with our principle) a number of smaller federations opens the way for advance. Some might be established before others. There is no value in uniformity of action unless it is also spontaneous. As nations long used to complete autonomy become accustomed to action within a federal scheme, they will become ready for the federation of the civilized world. (I am not a great admirer of Tennyson as a poet, apart from the shorter lyrics; but I am greatly impressed by the fact that in Locksley Hall he foresaw " the Parliament of Man, the Federation of the World " as a consequence of the invention of aviation—itself then very far in the future.)

Within each federal or confederate unit which is established the federal Parliament or Council and the Executive responsible to it will, of course, take over the control of all matters of common interest, including Foreign Policy. And secession would be forbidden. If any State which is sufficiently aggrieved by the action of the federal authority is free to secede, the system becomes unworkable. Abraham Lincoln was quite right when he insisted that to permit the secession of the Southern States was in principle to approve the dissolution of the United States into its component elements. Any federal government must have the use of full and effective " sanctions " against its own rebellious members.

But the federation of the civilized world and even

of Europe lies far in the future, unless this war, before it ends, causes such distress and havoc as to drive men to drastic remedies. Consequently there will be need for the more comprehensive League of Nations which shall include the various local federations. This, as the all-inclusive body, should determine the constitution of the Court of International Justice, and (if one be set up, as is urgently to be desired) the Court of Equity. What is to be the authority of these Courts —moral only or coercive also?

Here the lesson of experience is very plain. To entrust the application of " sanctions " to Sovereign States (whether themselves federal or not) is to court disaster. It creates uncertainty, which is an effective irritant. If it is possible, as I believe, to recruit an effective international Air Force under the direct authority of the League Council, and if the nations are prepared to agree to abandon military aviation as part of their own equipment, the League might have at its disposal a weapon sufficient to enforce its awards or those of the Courts associated with it. But if the Council has no effective force of its own, then let all mention of " sanctions " be struck out of the Covenant. Let us have no " sanctions " of which the application depends on others than the Assembly or Council of the League themselves.

The moral authority of the League may count for very much if it stands alone. But if there is, so to speak, a stick in the cupboard, all attention is diverted from a moral censure to the question whether the stick is to be brought out.

Besides getting rid of uncertain sanctions, either by making them certain or by abolishing them, we need to cultivate a stronger public opinion in support of League-loyalty than yet exists. On the whole this country has been a genuine supporter of the League system; but there are some bad patches in our record. It may have been so difficult as to be reckoned impossible to go to the help of China in Manchuria when Japan was formally pronounced guilty of aggression. But we might have avoided putting an embargo on the export of arms to both countries *immediately after* that judgment had been pronounced. That was a very severe slap in the face to the League's authority. It is pleaded that it was unintentional; but that only makes it worse. The action made it very clear that our Government did not regard the judgment of the League as a primary factor in the shaping of its policy.

In the crucial case of Abyssinia we took the worst possible course. We could, with some consistency, have refused to act at all. We had opposed the admission of Abyssinia to the League; that step was taken on the motion of Italy against our advice. When Italy proceeded to invade Abyssinia, we might have pleaded our former attitude and stood aside. That would not, I think, have been the highest ethical line; but it was defensible; and we might have retained the friendship of Italy. We took what I think the higher ethical line without counting the cost. It should always have been evident that no State should resort to sanctions unless prepared to go to all lengths, including war, to uphold the authority of international law. What happened was that we imposed sanctions to an extent which did the maximum harm and stopped before they could do any good.

We have not, I believe, been worse than our neighbours; but it is most profitable that each nation should pay regard to its own mistakes rather than to those of neighbours. The conclusion at any rate is clear and it is twofold: (*a*) no sanctions except under the direct authority of the League itself; (*b*) a new loyalty towards the League in the States-members of it.

One more illustration of the latter point may be given. The Disarmament Conference failed, and its failure was a major disaster. It failed, in part at least, because it worked under a formula containing two terms without ever deciding which of these was primary. The formula was *Disarmament by Agreement*. Is Disarmament the more important term? or Agreement? Clearly, Agreement. There is no more essential evil in a big gun than in a small gun. The evil is in the race in armaments. That is what creates tension, anxiety, panic. If once we can agree about armaments, we have taken the decisive step from regarding them as our means of injuring one another to regarding them as our joint equipment in the common enterprise of civilization. If that Conference had agreed to maintain the *status quo* for five years, without any disarmament at all, and then meet again, it would have taken a decisive step. When it met five years later, disarmament would have begun. When the nations cease to compete in armaments, and fix the amount of these by agreement, they will soon reduce their volume; the money is wanted for other purposes!

But to put Agreement first was really implicit in the whole idea of the League. To put Disarmament first was to follow the line of ephemeral national interest. Indeed the idea of the League implies that no State-member should take an action affecting its relations to other State-members except in consultation with them in the League. That leads us to the most conspicuous defect of the League—its failure to deal with Tariffs.

The League has done magnificent service in the social fields. Its medical work has been invaluable, and the International Labour Office, associated with it, has won universal confidence, though not all its recommendations have been universally accepted. All this work must go on. The League has also won great honour by its occasional incursions into the economic field, as for example its reconstruction of Austrian finance. But its activities on this side have been limited by lack of authority in the Covenant. We pass on therefore to certain applications of our initial principles in the economic field.

The way to be followed in this field as indicated by our principles may be very briefly described. We have to find a way of ordering life which

(a) expresses the fellowship of all men in one family,
(b) gives sufficient outlet to the self-centred acquisitive tendency in men to harness it to the common interest, and
(c) provides adequate checks and balances to prevent it from seriously injuring the common interest.

Of course that is easier said than done. It seems to me indispensable that States should consent to submit their Tariffs to the League and let free consultation concerning them take place. To impose a Tariff without so submitting it should be an offence within the competence of the Court of International Justice. Such consultation would of itself lead to many adjustments and generally to the lowering of tariff-walls. It would also tend to undermine economic nationalism which is an active part of the disease of Europe to-day. But behind all these contrivances is the question of motive in the economic world.

So long as we rely on the Profit-motive (as distinct from a secure but limited return on capital invested) as the mainspring of production, so long we shall be in a condition always verging towards faction within and war without. In the world we know, however great the need for an article may be, it cannot be produced unless it *pays* someone to produce it. If there is an idle coal pit and there are unemployed miners, even if they could pay the cost of working the plant, they may not do it unless they can also *pay* the owner. Supply of need is not now a sufficient motive; there must be also payment for ownership. We have reached a stage where that is become intolerable. And the profit-motive in industry and in finance, when given such freedom and prominence as it now has, becomes a profoundly and pervasively disturbing factor. The one thing that has become international in our world is Finance; it is arguable that it ought to have been the last.

Finance ought never to be in positive control. It exists for the sake of production. And production exists for the sake of consumption. The hungry and needy public ought to be the controlling group. Finance may rightly exercise a check, calling a halt to avoid bankruptcy; but for positive control it is functionally unfitted. Yet it exercises such control to a very large extent.

When we leave the realm of general principles for that of constructive action I have no qualifications to speak. Plainly we may cut the knot by following Sir Richard Acland in his demand for universal communal ownership. I shrink from this, because I think that the administration of the communal property would tend to become bureaucratic and mechanical.

But I would advocate a vast extension of public control of private enterprise; especially I would advocate a wide extension of the limitation of profits wherever liability is limited—a model scheme could be found before the war in the great glass-works at Jena.

I need hardly say that I attach no importance to my opinions in this field, for my special knowledge of it is very slender. I put forward these views rather as illustrations of a political spirit than as a political programme. If we could see the Governments of Europe genuinely co-operate in the enterprise of securing for the mass of ordinary citizens the full benefit derivable from the ease with which mankind now produces wealth, we should have moved a long way towards both prosperity and peace. But I am very sure that those who hope to see a successful termination of our present effort and the salvation of Europe from recurrent outbreaks must be ready for far-reaching changes in the political and economic spheres, and that these must be guided by the Christian understanding alike of the purpose of God and of the nature and destiny of Man.

V

EVANGELISM IN OUR TIME

BEFORE considering any question about methods of Evangelism we must recall the fact — the rather frightening fact—that the most potent evangelist for good or ill is the actual Church—not only the minister, but minister and congregation together. If the man who observes from outside sees no Christian graces in those who are inside, if congregations are quarrelsome or self-complacent, then no amount of preaching can counteract the harm that is done. The presupposition of effective evangelism, and the first step towards achieving it, is a truly dedicated Church.

When we turn to the task of evangelistic preaching we must still call on the laity. It is impossible for clergy and ministers alone to preach the Gospel to the detached multitudes. If they are to be reached it must be by lay witnesses. Their testimony is the more effective because it is not professional. The folk who are already religious do not discount the testimony of a minister on the ground that it is his job to give it, and they welcome the special help that should be forthcoming from one who is set apart to give most of his time to study of the spiritual life. But the man outside feels differently, and to him the lay witness is most effective. We must move nearer to a state of affairs where the minister stands for the things of God before the congregation while the congregation stands for the things of God before the outside world.

But we shall not get near that quickly; nor is it desirable that we should ever make that state of affairs altogether real; for there are and always should be men in the ministry whose gifts are chiefly evangelistic. In the days which are upon us we want more of these. Our training for the ministry has been too exclusively pastoral in its outlook and insufficiently evangelistic; that is to say, it has aimed at enabling men to foster the spiritual life of those who are within the Church, but has not sufficiently equipped them to make appeal with power to those who are outside.

In our approach to these we must in every age consider the frame of mind to which we speak. In one sense the task of the evangelist is always the same; it is to preach the Gospel, which does not change. But in another sense this task is different in every generation, because in order to preach with power the unchanging Gospel to the changing minds of men we have to find afresh the points of possible contact.

This is especially important to-day. We have to speak to people who attach very little meaning to the

word "sin" and none at all to the word "redemption". It is not that they understand what we mean
by these words and reject it; they do not attach any
real meaning to the words at all. A long while ago
Sir Oliver Lodge told us that the modern man is not
worrying about his sins, and we were disposed to
answer that this is quite true and is precisely what is
the matter with the modern man. But now the thing
is worse. The typical young man or woman of to-day
is indeed not worrying about sins, because the whole
conception is alien from the modern outlook.

We have to make our count with the mentality
produced by a disproportionate attention to natural
science in our new secondary education. Until the
last war our system of education was disproportion-
ately literary; there was urgent need to redress the
balance by giving a new prominence to scientific
studies. As usually happens in human affairs, the
reaction has gone too far. There has been an immense
development of secondary education in England since
the last war, and it has been predominantly scientific.
The result is a generation which has its standards of
belief provided by laboratory tests, and finds itself all
at sea among the imponderable factors which make
up the greater part of human relationships and of
spiritual faith or communion. We all know people
who tell us they cannot believe what cannot be
proved. Of course it is not true. Of course they do
in fact believe a great deal that they cannot prove—

concerning the trustworthiness of their friends, for example. But they enter upon the consideration of any novel problem with minds well trained in the handling of all that can be weighed or measured, but undisciplined and often insensitive in relation to all that is not susceptible of that treatment. This frame of mind tends towards a determinism such as undermines the sense of responsibility and leads to a view of all moral subjects as diseases to be cured, if at all, by the application of external remedies like change of material conditions, or internal but still not fully personal adjustments like those of psycho-analysis.

But this generation is at least delivered from facile optimism. It does not believe that the world makes automatic progress or that all we have to do is to leave it alone. It is profoundly dissatisfied with the state of the world. It can therefore be brought to some appreciation of what is meant by "the sin of the world" which is said in the Fourth Gospel to be borne and removed by the Lamb of God. Indeed this element in the Apostolic teaching is more easily understood by this generation than by its predecessors.

It is true that there is little sense of sin recognized as such. But there is a widespread sense of frustration. This means that we find ourselves unable to be or to do what we passionately desire to be or to do. We find ourselves in the condition described by St. Paul in the seventh chapter of the Epistle to the Romans. " The good that I would, I do not; and the evil that I would not, that I do." St. Paul goes far to meet the modern generation in disclaiming responsibility for this. "If the evil that I would not, that I do, it is no more I that do it, but sin which dwelleth in me." Substitute "complex" for "sin" and you have a very modern statement! Moreover, the modern generation readily accepts the view that a man cannot cure himself; indeed it acquiesces in it a great deal too easily. For it accepts this as an objective fact without suffering any distress of mind. It adopts the scientific attitude towards its own disabilities, recognizing them as facts but not feeling obliged to seek the cure.

Perhaps a perception of this obligation can be quickened if it is pointed out that the lamentable condition of the world is due to the fact that millions of people are as good as we are and no better. This fearful accumulation of evil is the product of our kind of character—generous, perhaps, with superfluities, but ruthlessly self-centred when our real or intimate interests are touched.

Our fathers had perhaps almost too strong a sense of individual responsibility; it led them to confine their penitence to that for which they felt themselves to be responsible. So sin came to be thought of as consisting of acts done in spite of knowledge that they are wrong. But sin in the New Testament has a far wider meaning than this; it is everything about us which is other than God would have it to be; it is all that falls short of the glory of God. The heart of it in man is his self-centredness, the putting of himself in the centre where only God should be.

If we take the sense of frustration and futility which is now so common as our starting-point, we shall be beginning with what is in fact a part as well as a consequence of human sin; if we can offer deliverance from that, we are bringing a true Gospel of redemption. The meaning of both terms can then be expanded to something more like their full historical significance, in ways which will appear shortly. At least we have here a sense of need and an offer to meet it.

The sense of frustration and futility arises from a feeling that in the modern world the individual counts for nothing in the greater events and can do no better than amuse himself in his leisure time. There has been something of this attitude to life in our own country. After 1918 it was widespread in Germany. The sense of community was gone. As Dr. Zoellner expressed it in 1934, *Wir waren kein Volk*. The great achievement of Hitler was to restore that sense of community: *Wir sind wieder ein Volk— Deutsches Volk*. Dr. Zoellner went on to say that Hitler had accomplished this in a way which made very difficult any solution to the problem, what is the relation between *Deutsches Volk* and *Gottes Volk*. He was a true prophet, and the contemptuous rejection by the Nazi Minister for Religion of his attempted solution of the problem broke his heart. I am glad of any opportunity to pay a tribute to the memory of that great Christian.

This widespread sense of frustration and futility in the modern world sprang from the lack of any personal allegiance to a community to which the individual truly "belongs" and which values the individual as a person. Men worked in herds at their appointed tasks of mass-production; certainly that is the reverse of solitude, but a mass or crowd is not a community, because in it the individuality of each man is irrelevant. In much modern industry each workman is no more than a part of the machine which has not yet been invented; when it is invented he can go. And outside the works, physically weary and nervously jaded by monotony, he still finds no real community. In the modern big town human beings are jostling atoms, and each must fend for himself.

Consequently there is a widespread hunger for unity, and it is by satisfying this that the new political religions have gained their hold upon men. In three respects Communism, Fascism and National Socialism are exactly alike; and these resemblances are more important than any differences.

(1) They offer unity in an effective fellowship. Communism hopes for the universal fellowship of the classless society. Fascism binds together the various interests in their several corporations and in

the corporative State. National Socialism provides the unity of Blood and Soil for those who belong to the same " race " and land.

(2) This unity has its focus in a Leader. Fascism has its Duce and National Socialism its Führer. If Communism has no similar title, yet Lenin and Stalin have occupied the same position in the thought and feeling of Communists, and the veneration paid to them is equally intense.

(3) Though the unity achieved rests on a genuine response of loyalty in a very large number, especially among the younger generation, yet it is imposed and maintained by force. The Communists won power in Russia by violence, and have taken the first steps towards a classless society by " liquidating " the other classes : the result, if it were possible that they should succeed, would not be a truly classless society, but a one-class society. It is manifest, however, that success is far off, for class divisions have arisen within the one class—as of course would be expected by any Christian who has heard of Original Sin and has acquired the wholesome tinge of cynicism with regard to unconverted man which that doctrine imparts.

Fascism limits the unity which it seeks to a single nation, and within that nation achieves unity by elimination. Matteotti was murdered, and there are many Italian Liberals in " the islands ".

National Socialism limits the unity which it seeks

to the (mythical) Race, and within that achieves apparent unity by means of the Gestapo and Concentration Camps. It also had its purge on June 30, 1934, of which the story is alone enough to stamp the surviving Nazi leaders as unfit to rule.

Is it possible to achieve what these movements aim at without recourse to their evil methods? Can we in our Evangelism satisfy the yearning for unity—for the sense of utterly " belonging to " something which claims one's services?

We must admit at the outset—or rather proclaim with all possible vigour—that at one important point the Dictators have an advantage. They know—Hitler best of all—how to win a whole-hearted response by appealing to what is best and worst in human nature in service of the same cause. Hitler appeals to all that is generous in German youth by his demand for utter self-devotion; but he also appeals to their egoism and pugnacity by calling for this in conflict with other nations; and he even provides an outlet for the sadistic impulses of his hooligans by putting them in charge of concentration camps.

When we preach the Gospel we too offer a unity of fellowship, more inclusive than those which we have considered, for it leaves none out; and we too name a Leader—the " captain and perfecter of faith ". But this Leader differs from the Dictators in two ways. First, He exercises no coercion and seeks none but willing followers. Secondly, He appeals only to what

113   H

is good in us—good by His own standards. Consequently we cannot at once offer a whole-hearted response, for a great part of our hearts needs to be changed before it can respond at all.

But He offers the one complete remedy for the sense of frustration and futility; and He offers world-wide unity based on freedom and not coercion.

The one complete cure for the sense of frustration and futility is to know and do the will of God. Everyone to whom this becomes a reality is at once supplied with a purpose in life and one which covers the whole of life. All duties can be done as duties to God and our share in the fulfilment of His purpose. It is quite true that in a world organized as ours is a great many people are called upon to do tasks which it is very hard to carry through in this spirit; and that is one main reason for urging many drastic reforms. But even what a vicious social order sets us as our task can be performed in the spirit of obedience to God, provided it be recognized that a refusal to do it, as for instance in a strike against bad conditions, may be made in the same spirit.

Christ calls men to the obedience of God by the way of love. They are to find their fellowship with one another as their hearts are given to God in response to that divine love which Christ showed to men in His life and in His death. It is a fellowship which is open to all men everywhere if only their hearts are open to the love of God. So St. Paul saw the Church as the universal fellowship where "there is neither Jew nor Gentile"—the deepest of all divisions based on religious tradition negligible; "neither Greek nor barbarian"—the deepest of all divisions based on culture and education negligible; "neither bond nor free"—the deepest of all economic divisions negligible; "neither male nor female"—even the distinction of the sexes negligible: but "one man in Christ Jesus". All are to be so governed by the Spirit of Christ that for practical purposes there is only one personality, and that His own. Each disciple so directed by the Holy Spirit becomes a member or limb of His body, carrying out his appropriate part of the great purpose. Moreover, St. Paul sees this Body of Christ, this one man in Christ Jesus, growing to fulness of stature as fresh races, nations, individuals are added, each bringing distinctive gifts, "till we all come—to the measure of the stature of the completeness of the Messiah".

We can see this happening before our eyes to-day. The Church is growing now, and for the last forty years has been growing, faster than at any previous period in its history. And where it grows, it creates fellowship. The true fellowship between Chinese and Japanese Christians at this moment is itself a most moving evangelistic witness.

During the last war it was found that no kind of religious address so deeply stirred the soldiers as one which brought before them the world-wide campaign of the Church. The story of that campaign is fuller and more moving now than it was a quarter of a century ago. Here is a most fruitful line of approach to the modern man or woman. We start from the misery of an aimless life in an apparently purposeless world, and for the desire to give allegiance to a leader and a cause and so gain significance for life. We offer as the cause to live for a truly universal fellowship and a Leader who appeals to all that is good in man or woman; and we show that He is actually fulfilling His promise in the world to-day. Then we emphasize the fact that He will never override the will of anyone. He will have no unwilling adherents. We confess that the Churches in all lands have failed in greater or less measure to respond to His call and truly to be the Church; our failures have obscured the vitality of the truth which we proclaim. Yet we know that it is the truth, and slender as our spiritual experience may be it is such that we can with assurance preach the unchanging Gospel as the message of salvation to this as to all other ages.

So we come to the essential evangelistic appeal, which never varies; it is the appeal of Christ on the Cross to all mankind and to each man and woman to be reconciled to God. "We are ambassadors on behalf of Christ, as though God were entreating by us: we beseech you on behalf of Christ, be ye reconciled to God."

At the end we give the old message. Only the

approach is new—the approach by which we make our contact and lead our hearers to believe that it is indeed their own condition, their own perplexity and burden, to which we offer relief. The approach here outlined leads to the heart of the Gospel. For if the offer of universal fellowship is to those who freely accept it, then the responsibility is on every individual. He is offered release from frustration and futility; but the offer is not unconditional; the condition is that he let himself be delivered also from his self-centredness, for it is that quality in him and others that makes the world a futile place. Yet that deliverance he cannot effect for himself. We point him to the power that can effect it, the love of God displayed to men in Christ; and we say, "Open your hearts to receive that love and offer your allegiance to Christ who shows it to you. Trust Him to deliver you, as you live in His obedience and companionship, from all in you that is alien from God's purpose for you, and so accept Him as your Saviour. Plan your life and fashion your hopes in His company so that you may shut out all that is discordant with the beauty of His character, and so enthrone Him as Lord of your life. Pray to Him for His perpetual strength, and adore Him for His holiness, and so acknowledge Him as very God. Thus you will become a witness to Him in life, and as opportunity offers in speech also; thus you will become a member of the true fellowship and take your share in the great work of extending it till all men are drawn in; thus you will find a meaning and joy for life in willing service of your Father and your Redeemer, whom to serve is perfect freedom."

VI

THE SOVEREIGNTY OF GOD

Thine is the kingdom, the power, and the glory, for ever and ever.—St. Matthew vi. 13.

So we affirm when we recite the prayer that Our Lord taught us. And unless we believe in fact that God reigns over the world that He has made, our faith must be very meagre. That God is the " Determiner of Destiny " is the least that can be ascribed to Him by any who suppose that there exists any Being who may fitly be called God. Somehow or other it must be true that " The Kingdom is the Lord's, and He is the Governor among the people ".

Yet while we affirm " Thine is the Kingdom ", we also pray " Thy Kingdom come ". For though by unchanging right throughout the ages all authority belongs to God, yet it is only too manifest that the world we know is not effectively subject to that authority. His sovereignty is not acknowledged; His law is not obeyed; His purpose is not fulfilled. If our prayer should be fully answered; if God's Name were hallowed, and His Kingdom come, and His Will done, in earth as it is in heaven—we know that all which embitters life would be gone from it, and all its perplexities would be resolved. For God is the Father of all men, and His loving purpose embraces the welfare of all alike.

Is the Divine Kingdom, then, something which will be actual in the future but has no actuality now? Assuredly not. In the course of individual lives and in the history of nations, God asserts His sovereignty by the judgments which follow neglect of His law. "Morning by morning He bringeth His judgment to light; He faileth not." When Our Lord looked upon the city that could not recognize or welcome Him, He read in that failure the omen of its destruction. The same nationalist pride that led Jerusalem to refuse its spiritual destiny would bring upon it the wrath of imperial Rome; and in its fall He taught His disciples to see the end of that age and the coming of the Son of Man with power. So it is when any civilization falls through repudiation of some one or another of the principles of Christ, whether that repudiation be shown in the maintenance of slavery, or in the denial of personal freedom, or in the clinging to such privilege and inequality as break up the fellowship of society. In every such catastrophe we see the Son of Man come with power. If Europe should prove itself unable to subordinate the selfishness of nations to the well-being of the civilized world, so that its rich inheritance is overwhelmed in the calamity of another general war—from which may God in His mercy preserve us!—there too we should see the Son of Man coming in power. Through the terrible anguish of such a time the judgment of God calls for a change of heart and action. If the new beginning is made on the old principles, it can only lead to a similar judgment. But if men will learn from the consequence of their self-will, they always can begin again in closer conformity to the purpose and the law of God.

We do not have to search by arduous reasoning to know what that law and purpose are. God has given to us the perfect expression of His character in Jesus Christ. It is to His mind that we must conform our plans and our policies if we are in our national life to ascribe to God the kingdom, the power, and the glory; it is for rejection of Him that judgment falls on us so far as we act on principles alien from His.

To-day,[1] at the beginning of a new reign, we are assembled here to give thanks to God for His guidance of our nation and empire hitherto, to acknowledge that the kingdom, the power and the glory in all the world is His alone, to dedicate our use of all His gifts to His service, and to pray that He will by His Holy Spirit keep us constant in obedience to Himself. If we believe at all in the Divine Providence we cannot doubt that so great and distinctive a fact as

[1] May 24, 1937.

the British Empire has its place in the providential scheme; its very existence constitutes our vocation. That is the relation of the Divine Kingdom to the kingship lately hallowed in the Abbey Church of Westminster, and to the Commonwealth of Nations represented here to-day. If we are both patriots and Christians we shall take pride in every aspect of the Empire which qualifies it for service to God's Kingdom; but we shall not hesitate to recognize that, being a human structure composed of human beings, there have been episodes in history and features of its policy demanding the repentance which is man's anticipation of God's judgment. Few things are of greater consequence than the grounds on which we take pride in this Empire or teach the children who are its future citizens to take pride in it. If the grounds of our pride is that it represents an imposition of our culture and policy upon other peoples whether they will or no, then we shall make it an instrument of our self-assertiveness calling forth the resistance of others till it perishes in the conflict it has provoked. But the ground of our pride in the empire can be far different from this; it can be, and surely is, the freedom of fellowship which unites the self-governing Dominions in freely offered loyalty to the Throne, the tradition and ideal of equality before the Law for the many races composing it, the maintenance of even justice throughout its borders, and the ready co-operation with others in the common tasks of civilization; if these be the ground of our pride we shall be vigilant to notice and to check whatever mars the perfection of our adherence to those principles, and shall devote our energy to keeping our great inheritance ever more true to its own distinctive character. It is not our power or will to dominate others that can be dedicated to the glory of God as we know Him in Jesus Christ; but we can so dedicate the good gifts of ordered liberty and freely established order, of equality before the Law, and of common loyalty to the Throne which is the focus of our fellowship.

The Kingdom of God is the Sovereignty of Love— since God is Love. That great proclamation brings comfort and courage to all whose hearts are attuned to it; for if God is Love, then Love is the ultimate power of the universe, and every purpose or policy prompted by Love—by the desire to serve rather than to gain—will reach its fulfilment, whatever the sacrifices that may first be required of it, because it is allied with the supreme power. But the proclamation that God is Love is not only a source of consolation; it is also a principle of judgment; for every purpose or policy that is alien from love and is based on selfishness or acquisitiveness is bound to end in disaster, because it is resisting the supreme power.

The Kingdom of God is the Sovereignty of Love, and the subordination of power to Love is the principle of that Kingdom. Once, and only once, Our Lord applied to Himself the title of King; that was when He identified Himself with the outcasts and the failures of society. " Then shall the King say unto them . . . I was an-hungered and ye gave me meat . . . I was in prison and ye came unto me."

Such a sympathy, including all in its embrace, has been the tradition of our English throne for a hundred years. Long may it so remain—a truly Christian tradition of kingship, which we know that the new reign will maintain and strengthen. Long may we all in that same spirit seek to use our imperial power to supply the needy, to uplift the down-trodden, to serve all men as their condition may require and our resources may permit.

Can we not look forward in imagination to an empire and a world guided by such principles? We seem to see a vast multitude drawn from all races and from every social class pledged to one thing and to one thing only, the acknowledgment of God's sovereignty by obedience to His purpose in every department of life. As they labour there takes shape a world, much like our own and yet how different! Still city and country life with all their manifold pursuits and interests, but no leading into captivity and no complaining in our streets; still richer and poorer, but no thoughtless luxury, no grinding destitution; still sorrow, but no bitterness; still failure, but no oppression; still priest and people, yet both alike unitedly presenting before the eternal Father the one true sacrifice of dedicated life—the Body broken and the Blood outpoured; still Church and World, yet both together celebrating unintermittently that divine service which is the service of mankind.

Such a vision may be prophecy if we will have it so; the condition to be fulfilled by us, who now thank God for our King and Queen and for their coronation, and seek to dedicate this Empire to His service, is that in heart and policy and act we fully acknowledge the Sovereignty of God. "Thine is the kingdom, the power, and the glory, for ever and ever. Amen."